BREATHE FREEDOM

BREATHE FREEDOM

The John McNeil Story

John McNeil

With a Foreword by
Benjamin Todd Jealous

ISBN 978-0-578-48191-3

Library of Congress Control Number 2019907337

For information on speaking engagements or to order
more copies of this book, contact justice4jm@gmail.com
or visit www.justice4johnmcneil.com.

Cover photo courtesy of Drew C. Wilson/
The Wilson Times.

To Anita

Contents

Foreword

This is a story about injustice, redemption and ultimately resurrection.

John McNeil's story is many things—a picture of America's broken criminal justice system, but also a story about the triumph of community organizing. John was arrested for defending his son and his home against a man wielding a knife—and charged with murder at a time when **STAND YOUR GROUND** laws were being used across the country to shield people accused of shooting unarmed black boys and men.

The story of what happened next is tragic: John was sentenced to life in prison after a trial that featured conflicting eyewitness accounts and all sorts of doubts. He spent several years behind bars and missed out on important moments in his family's life. It was a reminder that when it comes to protecting your home and your family, there is no law that can protect a black man from a biased system of justice.

But it is also the story of great triumphs. When I first worked on John's case, I was president and CEO of the National Association for the Advancement of Colored People (NAACP), and our North Carolina chapter was leading a political battle to return John to his family. That campaign, like any successful organizing campaign, started with a small group of people: John's wife and family, who persisted in drawing attention to the cause. John's wife passed away before he was freed, but ultimately, when he left prison in 2013, it was the triumph of a woman who fought for justice with her last breath.

In the end, this is the story of a man who, like Job, lost everything he had and then received the chance to rebuild his life and regain some of what he lost. It is a story of resilience and a reminder of the stark injustices of America and the inherent danger in our ongoing fixation with the gun.

John McNeil's deep and abiding faith in the criminal justice system inspired me. I hope it inspires others as well.

—Benjamin Todd Jealous

Interview with Frank Jones

Mr. Frank Jones is a local businessman who has known John McNeil since John was five years old. According to Mr. Jones, John has always been a nice and a respectable young man and comes from a nice and a respectable family. John didn't get into any trouble and has always been kind.

John was an athlete. He played basketball; in fact, John was a high school All-American basketball player. John had many offers to go to various colleges. He was what the University of Pittsburgh called a "blue chipper," which means that John was one of the top basketball players in 1986. John's coach, Harvey Reid, kept telling him that his GPA would offset the SAT score, but that was not true. Mr. Jones tried to explain to John that colleges relied on SAT scores, not just the GPA, in order to determine who got accepted into college, but John was very close to his coach and did not want to listen to Mr. Jones. The day that John was to leave to go to Pennsylvania, his coach told him that he wasn't able to go—if he did, he would be "redshirted," which meant he wouldn't play the first year—and had to go to a junior college. Needless to say, John was very disappointed. He decided to exchange his ticket from Pittsburgh, Pennsylvania, to Allegany Junior College in Maryland. While away, John's father and brother passed away. It affected him deeply, and he dropped out of school.

Mr. Jones continuously encouraged John to go back to school. Eventually John decided to go back to school and went to Chowan Junior College, then to Elizabeth City State University. He received his degree from Elizabeth City State University.

John started working in Atlanta as a salesman for construction equipment, mar-

ried his childhood sweetheart, Anita, and they had two sons, John McNeil II and La'Ron McNeil. They then moved to Powder Springs, Georgia, where they bought their first home. Later, they moved to Kennesaw, Georgia, to have a home built. In Kennesaw, Georgia, it is against the law to NOT own a weapon.

This is where John and his family's life changed drastically. John had a contractor, Brian Epp, to complete the work on the home that he had built. Epp did not complete the work in a timely manner and was forbidden to come onto the property. While John and his wife were out shopping for items for their open house and fundraiser for breast cancer, they left their youngest son La'Ron home to be there for the utility companies to turn on everything. Epp showed up on the property and started digging. La'Ron asked Epp who he was and Epp told him that it was his house and told La'Ron, "Nigga, I will slit your throat!" At this point, La'Ron called John and told him what happened. John told La'Ron to go into the house until he got *home. John hung up with La'Ron and called the police as he was on his way back home. During the call, John made a comment that he would "whip his (Epp's) ass!" The 911 operator instructed John to stay put, wait for the police, and not to approach Epp. When John arrived home, Epp saw him and picked something up from under his seat and came towards John. John loaded his gun as Epp charged him with what John believed was a weapon. John issued verbal warnings and fired a warning shot into the ground in front of Brian Epp, who continued his charge. As his attacker came within arm's length, John fired a fatal shot.*

A young white male, Bobby Smith, who lived across the street, witnessed the entire scene and stated that Epp charged at John and that John acted in self-defense. When the police arrived, they did not press charges against John. They agreed that it was in self-defense. John had no criminal history.

Nine months later, John was charged. The police testified on John's behalf, but he was sentenced to life in prison. John's lawyer filed an appeal. They went before the parole board. The parole board had options to release John, but they didn't. The appellate court attorney was to get the judge to overturn the case but waited until the last day to deny it. In the meantime, John's wife was dying from cancer.

"Back in 2006, McNeil was convicted and sentenced to life in prison despite arguing that he shot Epp in self-defense. The case sparked national attention over the **STAND YOUR GROUND** *law and how it is applied to Blacks and Whites who use it as their legal defense. Last fall, a judge ruled that he deserved a new trial because his original attorney did not inform jurors they could acquit him if he shot in defense of his home or his son.* **STAND YOUR GROUND** *can apply to the defense of someone else as well as himself." (Source: newsone.com)*

In order for John to be released, he had to plead guilty to voluntary manslaughter. In February 2013, John was released from prison. Since he had already served six years, John was placed on probation for thirteen years. He will serve his probation in North Carolina. Unfortunately, John's mother died July 2012 and his wife died one week before he was released. Sadly, he never got a chance to see either of them before they passed away.

Mr. Jones and John are still in touch with each other. Presently, John is moving forward with his life. He is doing some paralegal work, has remarried, and is in school to pursue his master's degree in school administration.

—Frank Jones, interviewed by Tamara Chandler

Chapter 1: Who Me?

I am not typically the kind of guy who is targeted for prison. Now, please don't get me wrong. I do not and have never thought I am better than the next person. I am acutely aware of the large numbers of men of color that overwhelmingly make up the prison population and are on probation in the United States. I have lived it and am still living it. I am not the typical African-American male that is earmarked for incarceration. The young men that are marked are usually uneducated or undereducated, have been labeled in school, come from single-parent families, live in poverty, and have no male role model in their lives. Many have had run-ins with law enforcement at a young age because they live in communities where poor people are targeted by police.

Scores of young African-American and Latino men and women, and poor whites as well, never stand a chance at reaching dreams. They are born too disadvantaged to ever catch up. "We hold these truths to be self-evident, that all men are created equal" is what the Declaration of Independence tells us. But there is no dispute that a person born in poverty has not been born equal to a wealthy person in America. To make it through the sinking sand of poverty takes extraordinary circumstances.

A young person who is rich can avoid prison because of the social capital and the financial status of their family. Social capital is simply who you know and who knows you. That wealthy young person will get an attorney who will not allow a plea bargain, even if the client is guilty. A young person whose family has money may never see the inside of a courtroom. But a young person whose family has no money and is accused of a crime will have to fight for their life. Even if they are not guilty, with attorney's advice they may plead guilty to a crime they have not committed. God may have created us equal, but people have a different system, making the wealthy more equal than those who are poor.

My family was not rich by any means. I was born and raised in a little town on the I-95 corridor called Wilson, North Carolina, about an hour east of Raleigh. I lived on a street so small in the black community they named the street Narrow Way. In Wilson when I grew up, poor people literally lived on the other side of the railroad tracks. Our county is not large. Back when I was a kid the whole county couldn't have had more than 50,000 people. We now boast 80,000 people. Wilson, like any Southern town, had its struggles with racial imbalances, and it still does. In fact, civil rights leaders in my hometown invited Dr. Martin Luther King Jr. to come to Wilson for a march on behalf of poor people. He agreed to come. He was scheduled to come to Wilson right after his march in Memphis, but unfortunately for us and the world, he was killed there.

Statistics show that many African-American families are broken, with only one overworked parent struggling to make ends meet—the broken family being a holdover from slavery when families were torn apart. However, while the stereotype is that black men don't stay with their families, the National Centers for Disease Control released a survey that said black fathers were present and accounted for in their children's lives.

According to their survey, black fathers ate with, diapered, played with, checked homework and read to their children just as much as white and Latino fathers did, and in some cases did those things more often than their counterparts. The findings from the study were published in an online article on the Daily Kos website in May 2015.

Men being present was also true in my family. Both of my loving parents were present and accounted for. My brothers Robert, Chris, Edward, Ronald and I had wonderful

African-American role models like my father and grandfather who were living examples of honor, loyalty, hard work, love for family and strong faith in God, the master of the universe. In addition to that, I had the privilege of playing basketball with a legendary coach, Harvey Reid, who set the bar high for all the players. Reid had such standards that whites in Wilson could not help but respect him. To this day his name is honored and respected by everyone.

As a kid I didn't think about racism or poverty. I just knew I had to obey my parents and do what they said. None of my siblings had ever had any trouble with law enforcement. We had good role models and strong sense of family and law and order, although we didn't have a lot of money. So, prison was not in my view at all, but I was to be given a life sentence in one of the strangest criminal cases the South has ever seen. I don't believe there has ever been any other time any African-American man could say that he had all white witnesses, including a policeman, to testify in court on his behalf. I also do not believe that there was any other time when police went against the district attorney in favor of an African-American male. All of the witnesses said I did what any father would do in a situation where a man threatened my son, and later threatened me with a weapon at my own home.

The facts of the case did not matter. The only thing that mattered is that I am black, he was white and that a white man was dead in my backyard and we were in Georgia. There was no consideration that in Georgia there is a **STAND YOUR GROUND** law. It was not even considered that according to that law you only have to feel threatened to protect yourself. The homeowner didn't have to actually see a weapon from the other person. More interesting, in the town of Kennesaw, there was a law that states all heads of households should have a gun and ammunition. They clearly never expected that the person who had the right to stand his ground and protect his family would be a black man and the man attacking would be white.

Growing up I was proud to do the right thing as I was taught by my parents. Not that I didn't make mistakes. Who doesn't? But I never engaged in illegal activities. I never did drugs or sold drugs. I didn't steal. I went to college and got a bachelor's degree. My wife and I were very young parents, so I moved my family to Atlanta for better opportunities careerwise. I was a family man with a lovely wife and two handsome young boys. I learned while playing basketball to play hard and play to win. That is what I went to Atlanta to do—work hard and take no prisoners.

I worked hard and achieved top status making business deals that put my company at the top in the Southeast. Many of my bonus checks were five figures. It was not a big deal for me at that time to get a $25,000 bonus check. I worked hard for it. As a matter of a fact, just before I was sentenced to prison, I had just landed a $197,000,000 deal building a Walmart that every builder in Georgia, South Carolina and Florida wanted. But I landed the deal.

My wife, Anita, was making $80,000 a year. We had both feet firmly planted in middle class. We had just had our dream house built in Kennesaw—six bedrooms, six bathrooms, two kitchens. There was nothing to even hint that my life would make a complete about-face. My wife and I each drove a Mercedes Benz. We wore Rolex watches. My suits were designer and my wife wore the finest clothes and jewelry. Our sons were well groomed and dressed nicely as well.

I never believed I would be enslaved and thrown in the bowels of hell—left to die there. In prison I lost everything: the house, cars, jewelry, status and trust in the judicial system. Most importantly, I lost my first love, Anita, and my dear mother. Neither can ever be replaced. My heart aches when I think about it.

What would cause such a set of circumstances? The simple answer is the complicated issue of racism in America. My enslavement was like many others in America before me and unfortunately will continue after me.

Never in a million years would I ever have wanted to go to prison. But since I have been there, I can say my life will never be the same. Prison changes everything about you. It shakes the very soul and causes you to change how you think. Trust is just out of the question. Everyone is suspect—prison administration and inmates alike. Nothing can be taken for granted, not even sleep. Men die while sleeping in prison. People lose all that makes them human. They lose their heart and become empty only to be filled with hopelessness, anger and doubt. Guards, who are supposedly there to uphold the law, break the law in prison.

Many times, people watch those television shows where guards will shake prisoners' bunks down. They say they are looking for illegal drugs and contraband. What most watching those television shows don't realize is that the guards know where to look because they are the ones who brought it in and sold it to the inmates. Think about it. How else do drugs get into prison?

Visitors are watched and searched. Bringing anything into a prison means going to prison. I know there are those who try to bring in contraband to their loved ones, but they are usually caught. Mail is examined. Guards bring in cigarettes, drugs, cell phones—you name it. The cell phone scam is one that should make all Americans shake their heads.

Phones are a connection to families and the outside world; they are needed to connect with humanity. There is no humanity in prison. We need to be able to know how our cases are going, how our families are doing, to hear the voice of someone who loves us. The voice of my wife was hope. I would hang on to every word she said. Guards sell those phones to inmates for a hundred times their value. Then they punish inmates for having the phone after selling it to them.

I had not given a lot thought to people in prison before I was falsely arrested and sentenced to prison for the rest of my life. It wasn't that I didn't know that innocent people were in prison, because I did know that. I was aware.

But I didn't give it a lot of thought. If somebody had asked me, I probably would have said something insensitive—for example, "Don't do the crime if you don't want to do the time." After spending years behind bars, I realized in a more poignant way that to be in prison is to be enslaved. Not just in metaphor but in reality. Most Americans are not focused on the rights of those who are in prison. Many would say if you are in prison you shouldn't have any rights. In many cases those who are in prison are forgotten. Society throws away people in a place where they can't be seen or heard from. Well-meaning people come to prison to have church with inmates and ignore the conditions of the prison. They are just there to ease their own conscience and say they brought the word of God to those inside. Somehow God never moves on them to look around and listen. But they have missed the mark. In fact, America has missed the mark. Americans sit comfortably on the fact that they believe the Thirteenth Amendment of the Constitution abolished slavery way back in 1865. That Amendment only prevents people from being born into slavery. Slavery never ended in America. The Thirteenth Amendment clearly states that slavery and indentured servitude is abolished except when a person is duly convicted of a felony. That should be a conflict for all Americans.

Knowing inmates are slaves should make anyone with a moral compass uncomfortable. If you believe slavery is wrong, then it is wrong under every circumstance. Even for those convicted of a felony.

In addition, we can't look at the penal system and not see how race plays an important role in who police target, how the district attorney proceeds, how jurors are picked, who judges are and how long of a sentence is given.

Back in the 1960s there was often an outcry about all white jurors finding people of color guilty in whatever crime they came to court about. Today, all over the country,

it is not unusual to find all white and most-
ly white juries.

Legislators pass laws that target African-
Americans. For example, until President Obama
signed the Fair Sentencing Act of 2010, a
person going to prison for crack cocaine got
more time than a person who went for pow-
dered cocaine, which is the same drug. Poor
people, who are usually black, used crack
more often.

Racism has evolved and there are no
signs saying "white only" or "black only."
That is too obvious. Terms like "urban,"
"thug" or "at risk" are used to single out
what is perceived to be an African-American
lifestyle.

What I would love our white brothers
and sisters to know is that when they target poor people, some of them are included.
It is like shotgun pellets. It hits everybody
in the area. Poor whites would do well to
join African-Americans and Latinos in the
fight for justice for all people.

There is no way to look at our prison system and not see something is wrong. How

could the census say African-Americans are only 13.2 percent of the population and at the same time make up 80 percent of America's inmates? Even when you go to states like Montana where 0.68 percent of population is black, their prison population is overrepresented by African-Americans, Latinos and Native Americans. Does that even make any sense? For those who have a moral compass, does that not disturb your sensibilities? At least make you frown?

According to FBI statistics, most people are in prison because of drugs or something to do with drugs. The FBI states that in both black and white communities, drug use is equal, but in African-American communities where people are poor, there are drug sweeps. In middle class America, they are virtually non-existent. Poor people go to prison. Those who have means go to rehabilitation centers. I do believe that in poor communities that old people, children and neighbors should be able to sit on their porches without gunfire. Drugs bring violence. We can't overlook that, but I am say-

ing too often law enforcement officers grab
low-hanging fruit. As I share my particular
circumstances about my enslavement in
Georgia, I hope America will consider those
who are slaves across this great country of
ours.

Chapter 2: Basketball and Life and More Basketball

I actually learned how to play basketball when I was just a young kid. And I learned a lot about life from my basketball experiences with coaches, other team members and my father. Many of those lessons I keep and use now because they have proven to be true.

There is the game you learn. Knowing the rules of the game doesn't let you play. A person can know the rules and just watch the game in the stands. To be a player you have to know the rules and how to execute the game. It takes dedication and hard work to be good. You learn, or I learned, that the game isn't easy when you want to win.

I learned there is more than just playing the game on the court. Being in the game also means living your life off of the court so your team can count on you. I learned that lesson from my father. When I was learning that lesson, I had no idea what my father was teaching me. I found the jewels of knowledge my father left for me to use in my adult life.

Basketball really started for me at East Street Park. I was a youngster and I used to watch the guys play, and, man, those guys could play. We had some true athletes here in Wilson County. I enjoyed watching them play ball and I would sit there and watch them play. I wasn't the only person there for that kind of neighborhood entertainment. The whole community came out on their steps and porches to cheer and talk about whoever was playing. It wasn't a fancy park, but just a park in a neighborhood of middle-class people.

One day they didn't have enough players for a team. I think it was one of the Hook's guys who looked around and saw me sitting there. I was a tall, skinny kid. I was six feet tall when I was only thirteen years old. Back then I ate up everything in the house, and I played ball.

I didn't know Tony Hooks would invite me to come play with them. That is like the coolest thing ever when you're just a kid. I was as tall as they were and even taller than some of them who were playing.

"Come on, young blood," the Hooks guy said. "We want you to play."

I was only in the seventh grade, but I was playing eighth-grade basketball, and they wanted to see if what they were hearing was right or not. So, I became a team member with the older guys. It got to the place where they would come down to the house and knock on my door. "Hey, come on, John, we need one," Hooks would say to me. And it all seemed urgent when he came to the door. It is always an emergency when you are a kid and the other kids want you to play ball with them. I remember one time I got a whipping at the East Street

Park because my dad got home and I was playing ball. I just had that one last play to make, and I looked up and saw my dad.

There were people everywhere. Back then the neighborhood games were a source of entertainment. Adults, kids, anybody and everybody came out to see the games.

But when I looked up and saw my dad, I said, Uh-oh. I knew he would not care that I would be embarrassed. I did not understand it at the time, but he was teaching me then to go by the rules. Don't allow your fun to come before your responsibilities. I had let the rules take second place to what I wanted to do. I didn't mean to, but that was no excuse.

I knew I was going to have to face my dad. He just pulled his belt off, wrapped it around his hand, and struck me a couple of times and I took off running. Boy, I got teased and laughed at for about a month and a half.

Now the next time I wanted to go to play basketball, I went back to Mom again with my most sincere face.

"Mom, they need me to play basketball with them," I said, looking as solemn as a church deacon.

My mom knew I loved the game and was good for my age. I know Mom loved me and she didn't want to say no. I kind of held my breath. She looked at me and said, "Ask your daddy."

Lord, that was the lesson. Dad was not going to be as easy as Mom. He was going to be tougher. So, I got up the nerve and went over to my dad. I didn't want it to be just wanting to play the game; I wanted him to know others were depending on me. My face was serious as I walked up to him. "Dad, I am trying to learn the game of basketball, and the guys are depending on me to be a member of the team out there," I said in my most please-daddy-let-me-go-I-won't-be-late-I-promise voice.

He looked at me and said, "No. Go sit down."

My most humble plea got me a "go sit down." I was fit to be tied, but I quietly went and sat down. I was upset, but I knew not to show it.

I was thinking to myself, I can't do anything I want to do, but I can't challenge him. My dad was six foot four and I saw what he did to my oldest brother, Robert. He tore him up good. I didn't want that type of action, so the best I could do was just sit down. At least I could sit on my rear end. Back then, our parents did use corporal punishment on occasion. Don't get me wrong—that was not a daily or weekly occurrence. They did a lot of teaching, but there were times when only corporal punishment seemed to get the message across to us. I don't know any black kid whose parents didn't use corporal punishment. Today folks say you should not use that and fear their children turning them in to the authorities. My parents understood they were the leaders in the house. We knew they were the leaders of the household. As children, we learned respect and honor. If my parents had not been the leaders, we would have thought we were the head of the household. That would have only caused trouble with our teachers and law

enforcement and would have been a disas-
ter. Of all of my brothers and sisters, I am
the only one who has ever had a run-in
with the law. I have to believe it was the
respect we were taught for authority. So, I
sat down sadly. I am sure, as hard as I was
trying, I must have looked sad. As a parent,
we really don't want our children to be sad.
But we have to teach them right from
wrong and how to go by the rules. "John, go
out there and rake the yard," my father
said to me. Now understand, this only
made me angrier. We didn't even have
grass. All we have is dirt. Why would he
want me to rake that yard?

North Carolina's soil is not like Georgia's
soil. Our soil is black. Georgia has red clay.
"John, take the hose and wet the yard," my
dad told me and my brother. Then he
pointed to the farthest part of the yard.
"Start at the end over there, and come all
the way here where I am," Dad said. "I
want lines in the yard." My brother started
at the opposite corner of the yard. We met
each other with those rakes.

I couldn't say a word, but I thought to myself, That is the dumbest thing in the world for him to have us do. Especially because my team needed me. What in the world is he asking me to do that for? Who wets dirt and then takes a rake to put lines in? Actually, why do we need this rake when we don't have grass?

But after I finished, it was pretty. There was art in this. The lines made the dirt look better than just dirt in a yard. We repeated this same dirt art for about two weeks. I really wanted to play ball and I couldn't go to the park. My parents were not rich. My eldest brother and I took a bicycle rim and made up a basketball goal in the backyard.

My mother had a part-time job in the tobacco fields. My mother rode in the truck to work in the tobacco fields with Mr. Jim. One day he came by and saw the makeshift goal my brother and I made. "I have a basketball goal at my house," he said. "I'll bring it to you tomorrow and we'll put it in the ground." We were glad for it, but we just thought it was one of those average goals. But when he brought it to us, we were shocked. It was super nice. It had a white pole and backboard with a nice rim and net. Because I was the basketball player in the family, my brothers asked me where I wanted it.

That is where I honed my skills—right there in that backyard. When I finished my homework and my chores, I played in the yard. I started making my moves and shooting baskets. My backyard skills carried to the East Street Park, then from East Street Park to Coon Middle School and from there to Fike High School.

After the two weeks of lines in the dirt, my dad said, "Go on back out to the park and play." But when I could not go to the park, I had my backyard. It turns out my backyard was the perfect training ground for me.

Chapter 3: Varsity

I've been blessed. Many people saw something in me from an early age. I was the first athlete in Wilson County allowed to play above my school ranking. There were a number of elementary schools, but Charles L. Coon was the only middle school for students at that time. I was in seventh grade at Darden-Vick Elementary School. They allowed me to play basketball at Charles L. Coon.

Mr. Crawford Lane was the principal at Darden-Vick Elementary School. Mr. Arthur Knight was the principal at Coon Middle School. They came together and said they would allow me to leave my school and go to the middle school and play ball.

The coach at Coon Middle School was Fike alumnus Gene Sauls. I didn't know what was going on at the time. Understand in Wilson at that time, African-Americans and white people did not have occasions to be social with each other. So I was surprised when a white coach would allow me so much playing time.

When I went to the eighth grade and was playing basketball, for the first time I encountered legendary coach Harvey Reid. Gene Sauls allowed Coach Reid to come over and talk with me.

He introduced himself to me. "I understand you are the new hotshot, superstar," Coach Reid said sizing up my ego.

I said, "No, sir, I'm not."

He looked at me and said, "That's OK. I like your attitude," Coach Reid said. "I've been here several times. I've been peeking in at you."

I was so shocked. I had no idea he had been watching me play. Then came the cool thing. "When you get to Fike, come and see me," Coach Reid said.

When I got to Fike High School, I was really excited. It was a different atmosphere. All of the kids went to Coon Middle School. But now in high school there were three schools: Beddingfield, Fike and Hunt.

The students I would be seeing in high school would be children from Elm City, Sharpsburg and other towns. They were kids I had never seen before. I thought it was interesting, but I was also thinking I would lose a lot of my friends.

My first day at Fike, I went to see Coach Reid just like he told me to. On the first day I was there early before homeroom and I asked them in the office how to get to Coach Reid. They pointed me in his direction. Coach Reid and I talked for a little while, and he started toward the gym. When we walked in the gym, and I saw all of the names of the guys who played varsity ball in 1982. I thought that was pretty cool. I thought to myself, Wow, my name is going to be in the gym. "This is going to be your home for the next four years," Coach Reid said to me.

I couldn't believe my ears. "My home?" I asked him, too excited to breathe correctly.

"Yes, you will play nothing but varsity ball," Coach Reid said reassuringly. Man, I was just a freshman.

I thought this was cool. I didn't know how these guys would measure up with the guys from Coon. I sat on the bench for the first four games. Coach would give me a little time here and there. On that 1982 team were guys like Bud Powell, Chris Ward, and Stacy Evans; now, Evans is a magistrate and a preacher. They called me Rookie.

The uniforms back then were nothing like they are now. They were short shorts; folks could see all of your thighs. When you fell on the floor, you'd better have on some good undies. You didn't want holes in them because folks would see that. Those uniforms were also tighter than they are now.

I remember we were playing Kinston this particular time, and they had some big boys. One guy was named Charles Shackleford who went on to play for NC State. There was a Tony Dawson who went to a

Division I school. Those guys were six foot nine and six foot ten. I was only six foot one back then. But Coach Reid put me in the games. He began developing things in me that I didn't know I had. The first game I played in, I noticed how tall they were, some big old boys. I turned around to take the ball to the hoop. You see, in middle school I could do that with little to no effort. I was bigger than most of those guys. But these guys were my size and bigger. They threw my shot out. "Don't come back in here, Rookie," one of the opposing team members said to me.

I wasn't used to that on the court. I knew I was in for a challenge playing ball with these guys. At the same time, it was wonderful.

When I look back on it, I can see that all those coaches saw something in me that I could not see. They knew that hard work would give me the physical endurance and strength that was needed for a championship team. I was just going on pure instinct. Coach Reid saw what could be developed. They were using my ability and my talent in a way I couldn't understand at that time.

I thought the coaches were the toughest guys in the world back then. Our routine was grueling and took a lot of stamina. I didn't understand and I thought it was inhumane what Coach Reid had us doing.

To start basketball practice, we had to start from the gym door, go all the way down Tilghman Road. When you got to the end of Lake Wilson Road, there was a stop sign back then. There is a stoplight at that corner now. We turned around and came two and a half miles back to the gym. We didn't stop running until we got back to the gym door. When we got inside of the gym, we walked around to cool down. The cooldown only lasted a few minutes. Then for thirty minutes we had to run figure eights or suicides before we start practicing. How many people could actually do all of that?

I thought the coach must be crazy. I thought many times of quitting the team. I didn't see all that the coach was building in us. But the coach wouldn't allow us to quit. When I got to be a sophomore, of course, I was still an underclassman and the guys I was playing against had been playing for years.

We were on our way to a game when Coach Reid told us that he would accept nothing less than a state championship. He used to tell me that I had it in me, that I could do it.

The night of the state championship, we were down by ten points. We were going into half time. We were playing against Roxboro Person High School. There was a guy there by the name of Avie Lester. He was a really big guy, almost seven feet tall. I had never even seen a guy that tall before. When you come against a guy that tall with a layup, it won't happen. That layup was for the little guys at Coon. Coach Reid surprised the team when we were preparing for the championship in a way that not even the college coaches I played for had ever done. Coach Reid had rolled down the goals and taken them out of the arena.

I stood there wondering how we were going to practice basketball with no goals. But Coach Reid had a plan. He told us we would run his plays on both ends of the floor until we got tired. Talk about pressure. I was an underclassman playing with juniors and seniors. He told me to take the shot, and the other guys were mean-mugging me. I passed up another shot and he called me to the side.

"Get over here," Coach said walking me over to the coach's bar. "Son, this is my last time."

I told him I had it. After that I took two or three shots. I missed them. I was nervous; I was used to other guys taking the shots. There was a big guy in the middle taking the shot. Now it had changed to me taking the shot. Butterflies. I was a sophomore in a championship game. We were down in this game. He looked at me. So? I looked at the other guys' faces on the team and they looked alike. My team said, "Man, take that shot." I had to believe in me. Saying it and doing it were two different things. After that I got hot. I ran the "backdoor," something Coach taught us, and made that first shot. I didn't look at the crowd, I looked at Coach and he didn't even look at me; he looked the other way. I'm thinking, I did what he said and I made the shot and he doesn't even look at me. Four plays later, the big guy, Avie, was waiting for me and tried to time it. But I could jump high and I dunked on him. The picture was in the paper. His big old arm was sticking up and I don't know how I got over that arm, but I did. At that moment, I was happy.

I knew two things: I could make a shot, and the Coach wanted me to make the shot. Add a cherry on top—my team wanted me to make the shot, too. Then looked up at the score board, we had won a state champion-ship. As a matter of fact, in thirty years, in Wilson County, there had never been a championship in the 4A ranking. Now the schools are 3A and 2A rankings.

I was the game MVP that day. That set the tone for other things in my life. I knew from that day what it felt like to go for the shot and make it. I knew one needed to have confidence in his abilities. I also knew whether it was my teammates, coworkers or family, I had to play hard because they were counting on me. I didn't want to let them down.

Chapter 4: Meeting Anita

I met Anita at the end of Narrow Way Street in April of 1983.

Anita was with her friends, Patricia Parker, Pam Hutchinson, Theresa Smith, and her sister, Melissa Smith. Melissa had a crush on me. They saw me walking. I was a freshman at Fike High School. I was coming from Little Bobbie's Store, where I got my first little job. They stopped me and said, "Hey, come here a second."

I was kind of shy then. We're talking about five girls calling me. I didn't know what else to say so I said, "Me?"

We were talking and Anita said, "I know who you are."

I said, "You do," trying not to smile and putting my best macho face forward.

"You've got some sexy legs. Can I touch them?" Anita said. She was flirting with me and I was kind of embarrassed.

"Touch my legs?" I asked her.

"Yeah." Anita said back. Now Anita didn't know that Melissa liked me, and I don't think she cared.

"Where are you headed?" Anita asked me. She was prepared to leave her friends. I guess it was every woman for herself.

I needed to make an exit, so I thought I would say the one thing that would allow me to go on my way. "I am going home," I told her.

"I tell you what," Anita said. "I am going to walk you home and then you walk me back home."

"What are you going to do about your friends?" I inquired.

"They are walking by themselves," Anita said firmly.

I started walking home and she followed me. I was kind of afraid of her at first. I had never had a young lady do anything like that to me before. We sat on my front porch. We lived at 113 Narrow Way Street. We never took the time to say both words. It was just Narway Street.

As we were sitting there talking, my mother came to the door and saw her. "Who is this young lady, John?" My mother asked. I hadn't asked her her name.

"What is your name?" I asked her.

"My name is Anita Dew, but they call me Toodie," she responded with a smile.

"Nice to meet you, Toodie," my mother said back to her.

All the way from kindergarten through the eighth grade I had never even spoken of a girl, let alone brought one to the house. Anita was the first girl I ever brought home.

"I have to walk home," Anita said. "Do you want to walk me home?"

"I have to ask my mom," I said back to her. I was only in the ninth grade and I had to ask permission.

My mother said I could walk her home. But it came with some old-fashioned questions. "Where does she live? Who are her parents?" My mother wanted to know. Anita told my mother who her family was, and I got to walk her home. That was something, as I look back on it. I asked my mother and she gave me the OK. I didn't have to ask my dad. Anything else I would ask, she would tell me to ask him.

On the way home we talked about basketball. She told me she played for Hunt High School. "I didn't see you," I said, thinking through all of the girl basketball players I had watched play.

"But I saw you," Anita said. She knew me. I just didn't remember who she was.

That night I met her parents, her sisters and some of her brothers. George wasn't at home. I met Darryl, her youngest brother. Through Anita I met and became friends with some of the girls in the Daniel Hill community, such as Sharon Briggs (Pooncy) and Solita. That was my freshman year.

By my sophomore year, Anita and I were going to be parents. Anita had been a virgin. I remember our first time.

When she told me she thought she was pregnant, I disappeared for a week. I didn't know what to think, because we were kids, and I only knew how to be a kid. She kept calling me. When my mother would tell me Toodie was on the phone, I would tell my mother to tell her I was busy. I kept trying to duck her because I didn't know how to tell my parents. In 1984 we won the state championship. My father told me I had to go to college and asked me what I was going to do to organize my life. And by that time Anita was supposed to go to East Carolina University (ECU) or Elizabeth City State University. Anita decided to go to Wilson Technical Community College.

Her mother was not happy at all. "You just let this boy ruin your life," her mother said. "We wanted so much more for you."

But Anita stood up for us even then. "No, nobody ruined my life," Anita said to her mother. "This is what I want."

"Well, you're going to keep that kid, because I'm not keeping it," her mother said. "I'm not going to do nothing for it."

"You don't have to," Anita said back to her mother.

When John II was born, we called him "J." Anita and I were only teenagers. We didn't know anything about life. We were babies ourselves. When I told my mom and dad, they were so mad at me. But my mom always had compassion because she was a woman. She had my sister when she was only nineteen years old. She understood what was going on.

"We're not going to leave her out there in the cold," my mom said. "We are going to do the best we can for the child, and for Toodie as well."

I think it caused Anita's respect to grow for my mom because she could talk to her about motherly things when she couldn't talk to her own mother. Her mother was so upset and hardfisted toward Anita about the situation.

Anita had a lot to consider. She loved me no matter what. "I love you and you are my everything," Anita said to me. "Whatever I do, I do it for you and for us."

I heard her, but I didn't understand it. She was far more advanced than I was.

Anita was eighteen going on nineteen. I was seventeen. She was almost two years older. When you are young, two years is a lot when it comes to maturity. Back then I really didn't do much. I played basketball and I went home. I was really a mother's boy.

Anita's family was not rich. She had to make do with what she had. Her family saw what a good mother she was and how hard she worked to make things happen.

Then in my senior year, she was pregnant again. Oh, Lord! The families were not happy. "The only basketball you'll be bouncing is on a job," my dad told me. "And I'm going to let you know something. You are going to marry this girl. We don't want all these illegitimate children running around here not knowing who their family is." My father and my grandfather used to say, whoever you have a baby with is who you will marry. All of my siblings were married. It was the value my parents had, and they passed it on.

When I went off to college, I thought a lot about my dad and my brother Ricky, who died of cancer. My brother was an athlete, too. My brother was hit on the leg while playing football at Fike High School, and he never told my parents. The area he was hit in grew and grew. By the time they took him to the doctor, it had spread. They amputated that leg, but he got worse. He was a couple of years younger than me.

I wanted to quit school. I wanted to drop out of Elizabeth City State.

"You only have a year and a half left before you graduate," my mom said to me. "You've come too far to quit. Even if you don't play basketball, go back and get your degree." That is the reason I graduated. Even when my mother wasn't around me, I could hear her voice. Mothers have a way of talking to their sons that always gets into their hearts and minds. Even if it doesn't happen at that moment, it was there. I loved and respected my mother.

Anita and my mother were the two pieces of my puzzle that completed me. God blessed me with such amazing women in my life. I don't look to compare other women to those ladies. Anita was a young mother with two little children and she worked at Pizza Hut. She even cropped tobacco in the fields, which is simply some of the hardest and most difficult physical work. Anita went the very first time with my mom to do it. When they left to go to work, they would be clean. When they got back, they would be dirty. And when you looked at the little money they would get... I would ask them, "You've been gone all day and only got $40?"

Anita was a worker. She believed in family and whatever it took to keep family together. She didn't just talk about it. She did it. How could you not love and respect somebody like that? She made me what I am today by just observing what she did. She always said from back when we got married in December of 1992, it didn't matter if she was right or wrong, we would never go to bed angry.

After I graduated from Elizabeth City State University, I said we were going to

Atlanta. My friends, especially Dwight and Ed McNair, asked what was in Atlanta. The same thing that is here, they thought. I felt there would be more opportunities and people wouldn't know me there. It was a big town and I felt I stood a better chance there.

Anita's mother said the same thing. "You're going all the way down there with this man you don't even know," she said to Anita. "You need to stay here." They almost talked Anita out of going. We had the U-Haul and it was loaded up. It was about eleven o'clock and we were about to head to Atlanta. Her mother was dead set against it. Anita asked me when I got things settled to come back and get her.

I understood she was torn. "I'm leaving one time and one time only—your choice is now," I said to her. "If you want to stay, I understand. If you want to go, get in now."

She told me to wait a minute. She walked in her mother's door, and in about two minutes she came out and got in the truck with me and the boys. That let me know that she believed in me. We didn't know what Atlanta held, but we wanted a chance. I had teammates who lived in other parts of Georgia. My teammates from Brooklyn, New York, decided to go to Atlanta. I figured I would go to Atlanta too and see what it was all about. I had visited there about a month before we moved, and my friends showed me around town. I didn't go looking for a job. Anita called me and asked me if I had found a job and I told her no. She gave me a two-week deadline and said if I had not found anything by then, come back to Wilson and we'd make it there. But I had already made up in my mind I was never going back to Wilson to live.

I'd been to plenty of big cities, but I had never lived in one liked this one. This city was different, and you could look up and see lots of successful black people.

When we got there, I got a job with IBM. I was going to be a programmer. I was the last hired and first laid off. A friend of mine was telling me about construction. I told him I was not about to do any labor. But

that turned out to be my beginning in construction, the beginning of some good
things in Atlanta.

Chapter 5: Mom

Edna Marie King McNeil is where my gentle side comes from. She loved us all. But it seemed there was something about me she took a little extra something with. I think she saw something in me. My grandmother, Sally McNeil, also seemed to see something special in me. Maybe they knew in the future I would need the extra prayer for what I was going to go through. My mom, who only stood about five foot seven, really cared about her household. She wanted to contribute to the household. She didn't go out and work a nine-to-five like they do now in the twenty-first century. She would go out and pick tobacco. First, she cleaned the house before she left. We knew not to mess up the house. It had to be the same as she left it when that truck pulled up out there. My oldest brother, Robert, and sister, Joyce, had things back in place by the time she got back home. When she got back, she had done a very long day of work. When she would leave early in the morning, her clothes would be clean and fresh. When she got back, it looked as if she had been playing in the mud. Her clothes would be gummy from the tobacco and were very dirty.

I thought surely if you come home as dirty as that and have worked all day, there should be a good payoff. I asked her for some money. She kept her money tied up in an old worn out handkerchief. Many people kept their money tied up in a hand-kerchief, not in a wallet, and when she would unfold the money, there would only be about $60 for all of that hard labor. "I know you were paid more than that," I said to her.

She looked at me, knowing I didn't under-stand how labor-intensive being in a tobacco field is. "No, John," she replied. "That is all we get."

It made me realize and be sensitive and appreciate my mother even more. She had to be determined to get up early and clean her house before the truck came at 6 a.m. to take them to work. They worked hard in an unforgiving sun to get that little bit of money. My mother knew there was a need in our household to make the ends meet. She took my older sister in the field as well. She also took my oldest brother. Somehow they skipped over me. Everybody went to the tobacco field except for me. We often talk about that today. They went out picking cucumbers also. While they were picking tobacco or cucumbers or whatever would bring in money, I would be shooting basketball. I guess they must have known basketball could be my way to travel and learn more about the world around me.

My mother made an exception for me in lots of ways. I never liked fish. Every time she would fry fish for the family, she would boil me some Red Hot hot dogs. One night my daddy saw the difference and decided to change things. "We ain't going fix anything extra," my dad said firmly. "He's going to eat fish, or he won't eat at all." My mom looked at me. There was nothing I could do because my dad had spoken. There was no room to make a plea about my not liking the fish. All I could do was worry about how I would fill my hungry stomach.

"Don't worry about it, John," my mother said to me in a comforting way that only a mother can do. We didn't have a microwave oven. She put a small pot on and boiled me some of those hot dogs anyway. I ate about four of them.

They were so good. Back then we didn't put ketchup or mustard on them. We would wrap a piece of white bread around the hot dog real tight and it would look like a pig in the blanket. Then we would go to work on it. I was glad she did that. I certainly would have been very hungry. To this day, I don't eat fish—fried, baked or broiled. My dad did cook on the grill. There was nothing my mother could not cook. I loved everything she cooked except for the fish and lima beans. She made the best meatloaf and chicken. Back then they would put spices and some vinegar in when they cooked chicken in the oven. It was so good it would just fall off the bone. There would be nothing but bones when we finished eating.

I learned to make that recipe, and I think I cook the chicken just like my mother. I recently cooked the chicken that way for my cousins who came to visit. I looked at the bones and said, "Great God almighty, where is the gristle?" Even the gristle was gone. My mother's recipe is just that good.

My family consists of nine members all together. That meant cooking at least three to four chickens, cabbage, boiled potatoes, cornbread and the works. That was dinner every day. Chicken was cheap back then.

We didn't always have a washing machine in the house. My mother would go to the laundromat. My parents eventually bought a washing machine. We had a clothesline in the backyard to hang the clothes on. At first my mother would hang out the clothes, but as we got older, she then took us outside to hang out the clothes. We all had chores. We were taught not to wait but to take care of chores right away. If it was my turn to wash dishes, my father might not remind me the dishes were waiting. He would wait until I had gone to bed and was fast asleep. Then he would come two o'clock in the morning and wake me up to do the dishes. Imagine, half asleep and angry, washing dishes when you could have been sleeping in bed. You learned from that to do the dishes right away. I do that to this day—take care of business first. It is the lesson after being awakened at 2 a.m. I take my hat off to my mother. She did a lot. The values she was taught by her parents and grandparents she in turn gave to us.

When holidays came around, the cooking was wonderful. The smell of the turkey, the stuffing, mustard greens, cakes—all of it was just a buffet of tantalizing aromas. To this day, I still cook mustard greens once a year. I only cook them once a year because it is a lot of work. There is so much sand that they have to be washed and rewashed. It takes so long.

My mom was a great baker, too. Some people can only cook food, but my mom baked and cooked. She made the best pineapple cake. She also made chocolate cake, which was not my favorite.

My mom didn't set out to teach me to cook. I watched from afar. I would be outside playing basketball and I would come in to see how far along dinner was before I could eat. I was really looking because I wanted her to hurry because I was hungry. I learned by watching her.

There were times when my daddy would tell me to rake the yard while I was waiting to eat. I would go out for a little while, but before I knew it, I would be back in the kitchen watching my mother because I was hungry and wanted to eat dinner.

So, I learned by watching. Then when I was in college, I used to call her and ask her how to make certain things. Now you know, you don't have money when you are in college. The first meal I cooked in college

was boiled chicken. I knew when the chick-
en was done because there was no blood.
Chicken and oodles of noodles was a meal
then. So, I would call her and ask her how
to make a boring meal taste better and she
would walk me through it. After I would do
a recipe a couple of times, I learned to put
my own spin to the way something was
cooked.

My mother was just a great mom and
beautiful to me. There was a picture of her
when she was young and I used to tell her
what a pretty mom she was. When I first
told my mother I wanted to move to Georgia, she begged me not to go. She told me
she had never been to Georgia. I went to
Georgia despite my mother's warning, because at that time I viewed it as the land of
milk and honey. The whole time I lived in
Georgia, my mother never came to see me—
until the trial.

I would send her pictures of places we
visited in the world, and I would always
bring her things from Georgia. The dining
room set I have now was supposed to go to

my mother. The one I had ordered for my home fell through because I went to prison. The dining room set was no longer important.

I talked to my mother, sometimes every day, during my second year in prison. I ran up her bill calling collect from prison, and it got to the place she could not pay her bill. So after that was handled, I got smart and I got me a black market cell phone. That allowed me to talk to my mom. She called me too. She just wanted to know what happened everyday. It was funny: she would always ask, and I knew there wasn't anything she could do to help me. But just the thought of her asking me how my day was and whether there was anything that happened she needed to know about made me feel her love for me. I didn't really know how sick she was. My mother had hypertension. Then she became a diabetic and had to take insulin. I learned later her kidneys began failing. There was a lot she went through. I believe stress also played a part in my mother's death.

When she died, I felt as if half of my heart died. My oldest brother called me to tell me she was gone. I was in Baldwin State Prison for the second time when he called me. My brother told me to sit down, that there was some bad news. I didn't know what it could be. I thought maybe one of my sons had gotten into trouble or something. Nobody thinks their parents will die. My father had died. I just thought my mother would live forever. It was devastating when my dad died. When I got the call that she died, I wondered what I would do. That was a hard call.

I know my mother is gone from me physically and spiritually. I still hear her voice. Sometimes when I am at school with the children or driving in my car, I think about things and it seems like I can hear her talking to me.

Out of all my siblings my mother said I have the quickest temper. Looking back, I did get into more fights than my siblings. I learned from my mom how to treat young ladies. She taught her sons how to be kind.

I think when you look at it, when a man stops respecting his mom, it wreaks havoc in his relationship with his spouse. As a matter of fact, I don't ever remember my mother raising her hand to hit me. My father would, but my mother never did.

My Grandmother Sally only whipped me twice in a lifetime. Once when I was young, my cousin Kerry and I had a fight and I almost cut my cousin's finger off, and she cut me two places on my leg. We were young and not thinking and I picked up a meat cleaver. When I saw my cousin's finger just hanging, and all of that blood, I just took off running. I am so glad they were able to take her to the hospital to get her wounds stitched up. You could never tell, looking at it today, what I did to her hand. I still have the scars she left on my leg.

Now, this is what happened at 141 Narrow Way Street. I knew I was in trouble. Instead of me going down Narrow Way Street, I ran through the backyard and went down Ash Street. When I got home, I crawled under the bed. My address was 113, and that was the only place that was safe, so I thought.

My grandmother came down there. My dad was scared of his mother; that is how tough she was. She walked straight in the house looking for me. She got down on her knees and pulled me from under the bed. She popped me on my butt good. I was hollering and crying. She put a whipping on me. She used a drop cord.

My mom and dad said nothing in my defense. I was wrong, and parents didn't take up for you when you were in the wrong. They knew that upholding you when you were wrong only made for a bad child. Children do things that are wrong, and it is up to adults to correct them. My grandparents and my parents had no problem correcting me and my brothers and sisters.

After she whipped me, she told me to come back to her house. "You are grandma's sugar," she said to me. "You broke my heart, but you are still my sugar." She had cooked some baked goods and I took my bruised butt back to the house knowing she loved me.

I was blessed to have strong, caring women in my life. I learned from my mom. I learned to keep a clean house from my mom. And most of all, I learned gentleness and love from my mom.

Chapter 6: Doing Business with Eddie Quarles

Everybody needs somebody to see something in them and give them a chance. I moved to Atlanta to improve the life of my family. At that time Wilson did not hold opportunities for me to move forward. I wanted the opportunity to take care of my family the way other American men did. I wanted to be able to afford to live in a good community with low crime, to be able to have a nice home for my wife and sons and to drive nice cars...the American dream. I'd heard that Atlanta was a promised land.

There are some people during their entire life, who don't get these opportunities.

It's all who you know who could help you on your way. Even in the middle of my trial, I knew I have been blessed with the people God has put in my path. I worked hard, but there are those people who saw my willingness to work and helped me.

In Atlanta, Eddie Quarles was the first guy who took a chance on me. He actually helped me to go into business. He was a businessman and he took me along for a wonderful experience. Actually, an experience of a lifetime.

Eddie gave me a hard time at first. He wanted to see what I was made of. In fact, he said I was arrogant and told me to get out of his office. So at that point, he didn't want to do business with me. I stayed positive; I wished him a good day and left. He was a lot shorter than me, so I wondered if he had a complex looking up at me, being as I was a much taller man of color. But I didn't think he was racist; I just thought he was being himself, grumpy. His company was Foundation Contractors, and he had the hottest company in the Southeast.

Everybody wanted to work with him. He was making deals with Walmart and anybody you could think of. Every company was trying to get in to talk with Eddie. I wanted to do business with him, and I was determined one day he would do business with me. One day I got a call from Eddie's secretary. She told me he wanted to talk to me, but it was at the craziest time I have ever heard. The appointment was at 5:30 a.m. I had never had a meeting that early in the morning. I'd started at 7:15 a.m., but not 5:30 a.m. I asked if she was sure about the time. "Yes, he wants to meet you at 5:30 a.m., and he wants you to be prompt," his secretary said. I always asked if there was anything I needed to bring, and she said just bring yourself. I could do that. I was excited when I went to bed. Everybody was talking about him and how hard he was to deal with. He just wasn't an easy guy to talk to. I wasn't sure why he was giving me the appointment. I hoped something good would happen. He had already flipped on me earlier and I didn't know what to expect.

I showed up at his office at 4:50 a.m. I wore khakis, a white-collar shirt, and I had a navy-blue blazer in my car. I didn't wear a tie. When I enter Eddie's office, his secretary was also there and I thought, Wow, he may be hard to work for, because his secretary is here mighty early in the morning.

When he came down the stairs, I thought, Here we go. He shook my hand.

"It's about time you got here," Eddie said to me. He always wanted to get a reaction from you.

I told him, "If I had known, I would have gotten here at 3 a.m., if you just had told me." Aha, I thought. Let's see how he responds to that. I had to see how he processed things.

"No, this is early enough," Eddie said, unshaken. I went upstairs with him. His vice president, John Almeter, was there for the meeting as well. Gus Sowas, the CFO, was there too.

It was a nice boardroom. I thought to myself, This means they have some money. I hope we can do business.

He showed me a project worth $50 million. At the time I couldn't see $50. He told me what I needed to do. He told me what the project was and to get with my manufacturers. He showed me the numbers where I needed to be or be close to. "John, give me your best shot," Eddie said. "I can't promise you anything. Get back to me by ten this morning," he added.

My heart leaped, but I had to remain calm. I was nervous, but I kept my composure. I told him I would do it. Wow! Five hours to make it happen. In my mind I said I would make it happen by 9:30 a.m. I credit Harvey Reid with that. Coach Reid prepares you for life after the game. My deadline would be sooner than Eddie's. I tell kids who are into basketball, be there mind and body, and when you get there, it is all about repetition. Don't try anything new. Whatever you were doing from high school to college to the pros—stick with that. It carries over to the work ethic. Always get there a little early. If the game starts at 4:00 p.m., be there in time to be changed and ready because the game starts at 4:00 p.m. You can't arrive at 4:00 p.m. and be on time.

Things do repeat themselves. In high school, Coach Reid yelled at me in the playoffs. I was feeling unsure of myself because I had missed three shots when coached yelled at me, "Shoot my basketball." Pressure.

Eddie Quarles said the same thing. Take the shot, or I can find another businessman who will. With that deadline, I didn't even drive anywhere. I sat in my car and started making calls right then.

You have to be careful on big projects because some vendors will try to change the price on you. I got it completed by 9:40 a.m. and went back into his office.

"What are you doing still here?" Eddie said to me.

"I got what you need, sir," I replied.

So he invited me in to look at my numbers. He never showed his emotions on his face. In fact, he knew you wanted something he had, so you needed to perform for him. He kept the poker face and didn't show me if he was surprised, but I shot the basketball. The ball went in the hoop, big time. Eddie went with it. That was the first job I ever did with him. Soon after that he had a couple of small jobs he passed my way.

The last job I did with Eddie was a major job. People from Georgia, South Carolina, Florida, Alabama, North Carolina and Virginia wanted this job from Eddie. People from all over bid on that job. It was a Super Walmart in Atlanta.

That...was...a...$197,000,000...project.

"Sharpen your pencil, you're going to have to get down and dirty," Eddie told me. "I like you, but I don't love you." He used to say that to me, meaning he had to be fair to everybody. "I don't want you to bottom out your price where you and your company can't make some money," Eddie said.

So, with all this going on, I could not sleep. I submitted my numbers to him. I was saying, What will I do?

I told the two owners of the company I worked for, John and Greg Crews, what I was up against. They wanted to know if I had a good shot at getting it. They knew I had built a good relationship with Eddie. "We are tickled pink that first of all you could get in to talk to Eddie," they said. "Second of all that Eddie would think enough of you to give you this opportunity when there are many salesmen who do what you do. If you actually close this deal, we will buy you a Mercedes of your choice."

When Eddie called me back, this time we didn't go to that conference room I was used to. This time we went to his personal office on the third floor. This was my first time in his office. His office had lots of awards and pictures of his family. He never was a guy who played around, but he punched me. I told him not to hit me. I didn't know he was about to give me a $197 million deal.

He asked me to sit at his desk in his chair. Eddie began showing me things on his computer and then he threw me an envelope. I wondered what it was. "Just open it up," Eddie said. When I opened it and I looked, all I saw was the 197 and all six of those zeros. I couldn't believe it. I was so happy I hugged him. I gave up my poker face. "You had better not let me down," Eddie said. "Everybody knows you're the big man now." I told him it was only because of him.

As I walked down the stairs, everybody began congratulating me. I had to be calm. Turns out my bid was not the lowest, but it was the fairest. I did close that deal. I sat in my car and thanked the Lord for that outcome.

I called the Crews brothers to tell them the news. I already had a Mercedes, but I wanted the SL they'd promised (and which, ultimately, they never followed through on). I got the secretary. I asked for John Crews. She told me he was in a meeting and asked if I wanted to leave a message. I told her I needed to talk to him right now. She asked me if it were an emergency, and I said it could be. I was persistent. I waited a minute and he picked up the phone. "Yes, John, what can I do for you?" John Crews said. It was about 5:10 p.m.

"I just want you to know I did close the deal," I said to him. "We did it!" He asked me to fax him a copy of the purchase order. I went to the nearest company office and faxed it. Everybody in Atlanta knew I knew what I was doing. I had good relationships with manufacturers.

Our company had this place in Loxley, Alabama, where we took people. It had full body massages, golf courses and the top of the line of anything you wanted. You could bring fifteen people. We took Eddie. The weekend cost $15,000. That was just a drop in the bucket in comparison to the business Eddie did with me.

Eddie turned out to be a great friend. When my bail was a million dollars, he posted the bond. He never hesitated. Eddie could not believe something so terrible had happened to me. When I got out of prison and was in North Carolina, I called him. I told him he should come to North Carolina to build another company. I made it my business to call him once a month and talk to him.

In January of 2015, he told me he was sick. He said he had colon cancer. He had surgery in mid-April. When I called him, he said he was in a wheelchair. Eddie said the surgery made him weak. When I talked to him a month or so later, he had to go back to the hospital. I knew something was wrong. Then I got a call from his daughter Stephanie.

She told me Eddie was being moved from the hospital into hospice. My heart stopped. I talked to him on a Thursday. It was like his last breath.

"John, you need to come and see me this weekend," Eddie said to me and he sounded terrible. Because of probation, I was unable to travel without permission. There is a lot of red tape. There was no way I could get permission that quickly. And I didn't have any money.

For me to go back to Georgia would have been a big deal. To go back to where I was imprisoned would have been scary. It reminded me of the life of Phillis Wheatley, who was a slave and a poet. Phillis Wheatley got to travel to London because of her poetry. Her mistress gave her permission to travel to write. Once she was in London, she found she was no longer a slave because slavery was not legal in England. Then her mistress got sick and asked for her return. Phillis could stay in London and be free, or she could go back to assist her mistress where she knew she would be reduced to slavery. Hard choices.

I loved Eddie, but I was free in North Carolina. He asked me to come back to the place where I was treated so poorly. I felt I owed Eddie and began making plans to go. He took a chance on me. He looked past my skin color and looked at who I was. He made a difference in my life. I was not ready to go to Georgia, but I would ask permission to go where I was held captive.

Before I could get permission to go to see him, he died. I got a text. "He's gone" was all it said. I was emotional. I didn't know what to say. I didn't know what comforting words to say. I called his phone and got his daughter, Stephanie. We weren't saying anything on the phone. I reminded her of the time we all went to Loxley, Alabama, and I could tell she smiled. She then told me he died at 3:13 a.m. "My dad really loved you," Stephanie said. "He thought of you like a son." I stayed strong during our conversation. But that Sunday it hit me like a ton of bricks. I thought about the time I went with him to Biloxi, Mississippi, and had rice wine for the first time. I thought about all of the things we did together. His service was at his restaurant on Marietta Square. Ironically, I went to trial on Marietta Square. They gave me a life sentence on Marietta Square.

It would have been difficult to be there. I thank God he allowed me to be in North Carolina and talk and think about him here rather than on Marietta Square. I miss Eddie. I have lost so much. I have lost yet another piece from Atlanta. I have lost Eddie Quarles, a man I loved and who loved me. Rest in peace, Eddie.

Interview with Minister Edward DuBose

Minister Edward DuBose is a member of the NAACP National Board of Directors. At the time of the John McNeil case, Minister DuBose was the president of the Georgia State Conference of the NAACP. He was the lead person in Georgia fighting for Mr. McNeil's release. The Reverend Dr. William Barber, North Carolina State Conference of the NAACP, shared this case with the Georgia State Conference because they were needed as a partner because of their relationships and resources in Georgia.

Minister DuBose believes that Mr. McNeil was found guilty of murder because he was a black man living in the conservative South, who, in self-defense, killed a white man. Those in power were not going to let that go. Minister DuBose also believes that if Mr. McNeil were white that he would not have served time in prison. If both parties were black, it would have been a case of one dead and one in the system, and the case would not have had the kind of attention that it received. They wanted Mr. McNeil locked up for life for killing a white man, regardless of the fact that it was in self-defense. Minister DuBose stated, "It's another example of a system that's not equal for blacks as it is for whites. What good is the Castle Law if it's not fair to blacks?"

The NAACP was instrumental in getting Mr. McNeil out of prison because they were able to help navigate finding and securing the attorney. They were engaged in a long campaign to "Free John McNeil." The NAACP put a lot of pressure on the political and judicial system. They were able to get the national board and the national organization involved and the state and national boards to put a legal team together. They were determined to have John McNeil freed.

Minister DuBose's motivation to become involved in this case came from reading and studying the case and what actually happened. He stated, "I couldn't turn a blind eye to such injustice." At this time, they are working on part two of this fight. Part one was to free John McNeil. Part two is to eliminate all holds and attachments so that Mr. McNeil can live his life as a free man.

As Minister DuBose worked on this campaign to free John McNeil, he got to know Mr. McNeil. He found him to be a model citizen, a model family man. Even while in prison, the correctional officers and prison staff found Mr. McNeil to be a model prisoner, and they didn't even know his story! Minister DuBose thinks that Mr. McNeil would have fought longer and harder, and would not have taken the deal to plead guilty to manslaughter, if his wife Anita hadn't been dying from cancer and if he hadn't wanted to get to her before she died. Ultimately and sadly, she died before he was released from prison.

"Although John has faced many trials, tribulations and obstacles in his life, he remains resilient! He has made it his determination to succeed in life. He has moved forward and will continue to do so. I believe that this book will create a conversation about wrongful convictions and justice for black men in America," says Minister Edward DuBose.

—Edward DuBose, interviewed by Tamara Chandler

Chapter 7: The Shooting

My family and I were comfortable. We were able to live like middle-class Americans. My sons were doing well in school and my wife was moving up the ladder in her job. We didn't want for anything. We lived in a nice house, drove nice cars and had amazing friends in our neighborhood.

Since I was in the construction business and I was doing fine, I wanted the chance to build a dream house for my family. We lived in an upscale neighborhood already, but I wanted that dream house. Anita thought our time in Georgia should wind down. I still had some goals to reach. I asked her for a few years before we moved, and she agreed.

Anita was my partner in life. We talked about things together and we tried to come to agreements together. I showed Anita plans for the house I wanted to build. She looked at them and didn't say very much at first. "John can we afford this house?" she asked. Anita was always very practical. This house had two kitchens on two levels. It was, by all standards, a house anyone would love to live in. I told her we could afford it, so she said yes.

At that time, our builder, Brian Epp, was also building other homes in that neighborhood. There were others who apparently had problems with him that we didn't know about. Epp built the home next door to us for a family member of his. Our neighborhood was all white, except for us. I never gave any thoughts about being the only African-American people in our neighborhood. There were many settings where I found myself to be the only African-American. I was not intimidated by being in those settings and it never occurred to me that being the only black family in the neighborhood would bother anyone else. I could afford the house and nothing else should have mattered, but looking back at that day, I am sure race, as well as the drugs Epp was on, played a role in his behavior.

It had been quite some time since the apostle of peace, the Rev. Dr. Martin Luther King Jr., had talked about his dream of his children being judged by the content of their character, not by the color of their skin. In his "I Have a Dream" speech, he mentioned Stone Mountain, Georgia. Kennesaw, where I resided at the time was only forty-five minutes away from there. Certainly freedom would ring in Kennesaw.

There were some things that needed to be finished in the house that our builder did not finish. We were trying to get those things completed. We were told to put the money in escrow, giving Brian a chance to get there and finish. He never did, and we got what we needed finished.

On December 6, 2005, we were in the process of actually moving into our dream house. There was the stress and excitement of moving and we were in the midst of it all. I normally didn't ride around with a handgun in my car. It was there because I was moving things from one house to the other.

I got a call from my son and he was upset. "Dad, there is this white guy in our yard, and he pulled a knife on me," he said in a panic. I advised him to go in the house and not come out. I called 911 and told them what my emergency was. I wasn't too far from the house and was actually on the phone with them when I arrived at my house. I could see when I pulled into my driveway that it was my builder, and I told the 911 operator that. I guess he was at the home next door to mine. The 911 operator told me help was on the way. Brian came into my driveway. I thought, What in the world is wrong with him to come after my son? He must be out of his mind to frighten my son and pull a knife on him in my yard. If he has a problem, he should talk to me and not frighten my son.

Brian came into my driveway and I reached into my glove box to get my gun. I got out of my car. I knew police were only minutes away. I told him to get out of my yard, but he kept coming. I repeated for him to get out of my yard and go his way. I told him that police were on their way. He kept coming toward me arguing loudly. I wasn't sure why he kept coming towards me. This guy was something else. He threatened my son. Now he was making me feel unsafe in my own backyard. Who does this? So in order to make him stop, I fired a warning shot into the ground. I warned him I had a gun and he needed to stop yelling and coming towards me in my own yard.

To my shock, that didn't faze him. I was backing up from him, facing him. I didn't turn my back because I didn't know what in the world he would do. I thought Epp might be there to kill me or something. I knew the police would be there any moment. I wondered, Does this guy think he's going to kill me? I wondered what he had in his pockets. Was he there to kill my whole family?

Now he was in arm's reach of me and coming in. I raised the gun and pulled the trigger. I didn't know where the bullet would hit him. I was not thinking of killing him. I was at my back door when the shot rang out and he fell.

Just as the 911 operator promised, the police drove up. Brian was dead. I had killed a man. I never thought in my life I would be in this situation. The detectives came up and began assessing the situation. What my son thought was a knife was a box cutter that Brian had pulled on him.

My son and I were taken to the police station. We were drilled for two hours. What happened? Why did I think it happen? Did Epp and I have a dispute? The police also interviewed an eyewitness, who corroborated the events.

Truthfully, I didn't know what happened. I didn't know why he was acting like he did toward my family and, no, I didn't have a beef with him. I knew he didn't finish the house, but he had the opportunity to do so.

After two very long hours, the detective allowed us to go home. They said I did not commit a crime. I was told if anything else should arise, they would call me. I went home thanking God to be able to go home with my son.

It was not a good feeling to know a man was dead by my hands. It was also not a good feeling that someone would pull a weapon on my son.

It was a rough start, but we were going to be in our new home and make some new memories for our family. I rested in the fact that the police and neighbors all saw I was not guilty of murder. I was protecting my son and my home. I am an American and I have that right. For over 275 days, I was home in Kennesaw.

Then on August 10, 2006, a grand jury was convened and I was indicted for malice murder, felony murder, and aggravated assault. I was arrested on August 11, 2006.

Chapter 8: The Trial

I was in jail until September 9, when Eddie Quarles paid my million-dollar bond so that I could come back home to my family—back to my dream house. But when I got back to that house, it meant nothing to me. It was just a building. It felt as if somebody had stripped me of everything. Don't get me wrong, the house was beautiful, and everything was in place, but nothing was the same. To me it wasn't home anymore. If you've ever been a victim of a car or house break-in, there is just an uneasy feeling. It was ten times as bad coming back to the house.

The house was beautiful. There were three levels with six bedrooms with a bathroom in each bedroom and two half baths. Two kitchens were for convenience: one upstairs on the main level and one downstairs on the basement level. That basement level was so that when we entertained we would not have to cook food upstairs and then bring it downstairs.

I still have a part of the house with me— the double doors where you entered. I have them as a reminder. If God blesses me to have the house I have the blueprints to, I want to put the same doors up to remind me of how you can lose everything. But in God's time he will restore you just like he did Job.

I got out of jail September 9, 2006, and the trial began October 30 of the same year. Between the time I was released and the time the trial began, a *second* grand jury was convened for the same incident. In addition to malice murder, felony murder, and aggravated assault, they indicted me for voluntary manslaughter.

During that time, I stayed worried. I was scared to death. I could hardly eat. I could not sleep. All of what happened took away my spirit. I knew my family was there in the house, and I didn't want to worry them. People say they don't worry about things, and that is hard to believe. When you have no clue what the outcome will be, you will worry. I have a testimony because I did make it out. It could have gone the other way.

There were so many things to escape. It reminded me of Paul, who came across the sea and escaped drowning only to be bitten by the most poisonous snake on the island. The people first said he was a murderer and then a god when he did not die from the snakebite. It turned nonbelievers into believers. In my case, Hannah Lorra, one of my cousins from Philadelphia, told me my situation gave her faith. She told me when I used to talk to her I would tell her I was coming home soon. Hannah said she didn't want to break my spirit and would not tell me she didn't believe it. She was looking at the fact that I had a life sentence and she believed I would be in there for the rest of my life. When I used to tell her I was getting out, she would just tell me to keep praying and maybe God would answer my prayer.

When you are sentenced to life, you normally do twenty-five years before you are up for parole. And normally when you come up for parole the first time you are denied and have to wait eight years before they talk with you again. When a guy would be up for a parole hearing, that guy would be excited. When they came back denied, you knew there would be a fight. You could feel their anger and rage in the air. It would not take much to spark the fire. They might come back to their cell and their cellmate would be in there. The guy might want to cry by himself and his cellmate might not want to leave, so they'd begin fighting.

When a guy would get parole, it gave other inmates hope. Usually they were white inmates. So, Hannah didn't see how I could possibly get out earlier. It did not dawn on me she had no faith that I could get out of prison. She went to fill a space at church every Sunday and Wednesday, but church was far from her. The spirit was far from her.

Had she had the spirit of God, when the word of God came forth, she would have received it. He said, How do you know the spirit? Test the spirit by the spirit.

We had a talk when I got out. "I have a confession to make," Hannah said to me. "I heard you, but I didn't believe that it was going to happen." That let me know that the spiritual transformation that God did in me was not just for me. It was also for my family and friends so they could see and so they could believe.

Because of the trial, my mother made her first entrance into the state of Georgia. As upset as I was, it was exciting to see her in Georgia. My oldest brother drove her down.

When she came in, she looked around. "What are you doing with this kind of house?" she asked me. "You don't need this much house."

I changed the subject. "What would you like to eat, Mom?" I asked her. So we ate and then we went into the family room.

She looked at me the way only a mother could look. "John, I am scared for you," she admitted.

I was already scared, but I didn't want to tell her. That was just confirmation that I was going to prison. When your mom feels so out of sorts and then she tells you, you can believe it. Moms seem to have an interconnection with their children's soul.

I used to have night terrors where I would be in prison and I would be fighting. I would wake up in a cold sweat. I would get up and go downstairs and sit without turning any lights on. There was no need to disturb anybody else with my fears.

While I waited for trial, I had time to think about the fact I was there because of money. I thought I was being prosperous closing all of those deals. We talked about moving to Maryland and I promised I would, but I was making good money. If I had just done what I promised, I would not have been in that situation. Now I try not to promise anything. If I promise, I have to keep my promise. If I don't, there are repercussions. I looked at Anita and my sons and I knew I had let them down.

At the time I thought I was achieving the American dream. Now looking back and thinking about all of the people I have lost along the way, I am not sure if it was a dream or a curse. During jury selection we didn't have one black male to put on the jury. There were two African-American women who I wanted to be on the jury. Jesse Evans, deputy assistant district attorney of Cobb County struck down anybody who looked progressive. They had to get rid of five people. I still think my lawyer could have done more during that phase. One of the women I wanted was married to a retired police chief and the other was married to a retired highway patrolman. They were firm. The two black women on the jury that we got had some kinfolks who were in trouble. It isn't unusual for black men from the ages of thirteen to thirty to have had at least one brush with the law.

The first day of the trial, I was dressed and ready and downstairs. We were all downstairs except for my mother. I had butterflies in my stomach. I looked up the stairs to see if she was coming. I asked my son John to go and see where Grandma was. As he climbed the stairs, I could see his eyes were filled with tears. She was in the bathroom on her knees praying to God. I looked at him and walked away. I almost cried. I pretended to be looking for something. The trial lasted eight days.

When we walked in the courtroom, my mother did a hundred-and-eighty-degree turn. She went from praying to angry. Judge Dorothy Robinson, who presided over the case, knew my mom was angry. Judge Robinson has since retired. She was appointed by then-President Jimmy Carter. The courtroom was filled. My mother stood up and began talking out loud when Jesse Evans would say bad things about me. He painted a picture to the jury that I was a monster. He called me a professional thug. My mom stood up twice and yelled. "That's a lie," she said loudly. She stood up for a while talking. He said he didn't care if I

was a homecoming king or queen. The
judge didn't hold my mother in contempt.
She let my mom talk.

I was on the stand and I was not letting
Jesse Evans get to me. My mother was angry and began talking again. "Judge, can
you make that lady shut her mouth?" Evans said to the judge. Part of me just
snapped. I was so close to him, I could have
broken his neck. He was standing up there
trying to be bad, not knowing if I was the
bad person he said I was. I could have gotten him before the bailiff could have gotten
over there.

I told him he was a liar during court.
When he excused me from the stand I did not
move. The judge had to ask me to move. I
could tell the white jurors were already
against me. Jesse Evans told lies about com-
ments I supposedly made. The judge asked
him to show her the comment and then told
him that was not the comment I made.

The jurors should have realized if Jesse
Evans lied about one thing, he would lie
about other things. I could see how things

were going during the trial. I would come home every day and not want to be bothered with anyone. I knew I needed to get things in order for when I would go to prison, but I just couldn't do it. I had too much on my mind. I was losing weight.

Before the end of the trial, Frank Jones came to Georgia. We had lunch while there was a recess. He left that day. He hasn't said it out loud to me to this day, but he knew I was going to be found guilty and have to go to prison. As I consider things, my mind was already locked up. My body was free, but my mind was in bondage.

It didn't take much longer than a half hour before the jury came back with the verdict. My attorney looked at me and I felt he had sold me out. "John we can come back on the appeal," he said to me. He knew I had lost the case. He said that before the head juror said the verdict. Anita was sitting there nervously crying. Eddie Quarles was there.

I was asked to stand. The jury charged me. The first charge was malice murder.

"We, the jury, find you not guilty," the juror said. I was shocked. I took a breath. I thought maybe there would be a miracle. Then the second charge of felony murder. "We, the jury, find John McNeil guilty," the juror's voice rang out. I don't remember what was said after that. I was later found guilty of aggravated assault. Fourth was voluntary manslaughter. I was found not guilty of voluntary manslaughter.

By that time everybody in the courtroom who was with me was hollering and crying. Some of the black deputies in the courtroom allowed me to walk to Anita and kiss her without handcuffs. I didn't get to hug my mother. Everybody was crying except for me. I was angry and I was scared. Deputies allowed me to walk to the back without handcuffs. One of the officers told me he knew what happened was wrong. I changed from the suit I wore in court to an orange jumpsuit. I went to Cobb County jail. They put me in a special cell where they could watch me for twenty-four hours. They feared I would kill myself.

After twenty-four hours, they moved me to the "A" pod where all of the people who were accused of murder were kept. I stayed there for three days until they shipped me out to Diagnostics.

The "A" pod was a battleground. The inmates there fought all of the time. There was fresh blood on the floor. People were leaking blood. I was just sitting and looking. It was crazy inside there.

The inmates were looking at me on the television and I was sitting in there. They knew before I got there who I was. There was a guy there who wanted to fight me, but we didn't fight. I knew the battle was going to continue.

My Lord, deliver me.

Chapter 9: My Father, Myself

When I was a senior at Ralph L. Fike High School in 1986, Robert McNeil Sr., my father, didn't get to see me in the playoffs or winning the championship that time. He was shot in the back by a man named Douglas Dawson. I don't know all of what happened, but the family's conversation is that Dawson was married to my mother's sister and was abusive to her. My father didn't agree with men abusing women and used to get on Dawson about his abusive ways.

One thing led to another, and, as the story goes, Dawson was drinking and started an argument with my dad. He pulled a gun on my dad and my dad took off running. He shot my father in the back with a .22-caliber gun.

We were home the night my father was shot. My brother Robert Jr. and I ran outside and saw him lying in the backyard. My mother called the paramedics. We didn't know at the time he would be paralyzed. We just knew he couldn't move.

I was so scared looking down at him. He must have known my fear. "I'm going to be all right," he said to me. I wanted him to reassure me, but part of me knew he was not going to be all right. The paramedics came, and my dad had to be picked up and put on the stretcher.

We would visit him in the hospital in Greenville, North Carolina. He had a lot of tubes going into him. That kind of made me angry. On one of those visits they told us that the doctor couldn't remove the bullet and he would remain paralyzed. I cried like a baby. I realized we had to protect him. We had to look out for him.

The anger made us want to get revenge on the man who shot him. My father said not to worry about what happened and to leave everything alone.

But my brother and I made a deal between us that we would catch him on the street and jump on him and beat him up pretty good.

Dawson eventually went to prison and also got out. A year or two after he was released from prison, he died of health problems. My brother and I never got the chance to do what we wanted to him. We understood that if we had allowed revenge to blind us, we might end up in trouble ourselves. My father died from complications from the gunshot some years later. My father died after Dawson's death.

My father's shooting and eventual death devastated us. We were accustomed to our leader. He was the one who set the example, and he set the tone. It seemed he was hard on us growing up. But when something like that happens, where do you go? What do you do? We saw this man we all looked up to go from walking around and being in charge of his life, going to work or wherever he wanted, to being helpless in a wheelchair. He needed us to wait on him hand and foot.

. I had come out of my shell and had begun to believe in people. I was trying to learn who I was and to figure out some things about myself. I was beginning to start to believe in my abilities. When my father was taken, I went back into that shell.

It was so ironic that my father died as a result of a gunshot. I was imprisoned because of a gunshot. We both suffered a type of paralysis. His was literal and mine was figurative, but we were both paralyzed just the same.

When they locked me up on August 11, 2006, in the Cobb County jail, it was frightening. I saw things I didn't understand. Two inmates hanged themselves. Inmates fought every day. Many times they were severely hurt. Inmates would get robbed for their store goods they had bought. Even though I was scared, I didn't know how much danger I was in. I didn't know I was at death's door. I could feel that something was totally wrong. I felt how my father must have felt that night I saw him lying on the ground. He was helpless. I was able to stand on my feet, but I was helpless, too.

Like my father, I was my two sons' leader. I had a wife and I was her leader. And there I was, defenseless against a wicked system where I might never get a chance to be that leader for them again. I stayed in jail from August 11 through September 9. I went before a judge who was appointed to hear the case. Her name was Judge Dorothy A. Robinson. She has since retired. She had been through some kind of turmoil in her life the year before. A black man, who was driving drunk had run a red light, smashed into her daughter and killed her. A black man killed her white daughter.

Judge Robinson knew at the time that I was not guilty of any crime. The records and the investigation showed her what happened. The lead officer, Detective Brad MacIntosh, was an honorable man. He went against the district attorney, at that time Patrick Head, to testify on my behalf.

I would like to look him in his eye one day and say thank you. I would like to thank him for believing in me in the worst ordeal of my life. He looked past the color of my skin and at who I was and told the truth. He didn't have to do that. I believe the God in him was so bold that he went against those he would normally unite with. I owe him that thank you. I want to give him a proper thank you. I was later told that my case was the first time Judge Robinson gave a bond for a murder case in Cobb County. My bond was $1,000,000. I had the choice of $450,000 cash or $1,000,000 worth of property.

My dear friend Eddie Quarles paid my bond. I went home to my house 505 Earl Vine Way, Kennesaw, Georgia, where the incident occurred on December 6, 2005.

At the time I didn't mind going back to my house. I thought I had done what any father or parent in America would have done. If I couldn't protect my castle and protect my family in this great place called America, where could I do it?

You see, there was a law in Kennesaw that stated every head of household should have a gun and bullets. That was in addition to the state's **STAND YOUR GROUND** law. There were two laws on the books that said I could protect my family and my home. In fact, the law was so clear that it said even if I *felt* like I was in danger I had the right to protect myself. Not if I saw a knife. Not if someone charged me. If I *felt* as if I were in danger. I felt in danger. But as an African-American, I was not allowed protection within the law under which my family and I resided.

Yes, I wanted to go back home. My family was there. It was my home. I wasn't at Epp's home or in the street. I was where I paid the bills. Yes, the incident took place there. Yes, a man died there in the driveway. But it was home to us. On the day of the incident, I underwent a two-hour interrogation. They said no charges would be filed. I went home then, also. But this was very different.

In August, when I went back to jail, people told me in jail they knew of my case through the media. When they were fingerprinting me and booking me, I didn't know what to expect. I was actually going inside this time to stay in the jail. I knew the environment was not conducive for me. I was strip searched. They grab your genitals. They make you bend over and they look in your butt. I felt violated. That frightened me and angered me at the same time.

They treated me poorly. I had a little mattress and I had to sleep on the floor. I was not allowed to have soap for the first night in order to shower. They didn't have washcloths. One of the guys allowed me to borrow his shower shoes to go in the shower.

In my profession, I was successful. I was accustomed to things. Anything I needed was in arm's reach. My wife and I used to get pedicures and manicures. In jail I was putting my feet in the shower shoes of some guy I'd never met before. I certainly had fallen from what I was used to. The second night I was there, officers kicked the mattress I was sleeping on 3:30 a.m. "Get up," they yelled. I mustered all the calm I could and asked what was wrong. "Just get up and take this tuberculosis shot," he yelled.

"Let me call my lawyer," I said.

"The phones are not on," the officer said back to me.

"I'm not taking no shot," I said back sternly.

The officer was white. The nurse was black. The needle was already made up. She didn't have to draw the medicine in the needle. I didn't trust that.

I told them I was not taking that. I told them I didn't know if the medicine had actually come out of the bottle I saw sitting there. I told the deputy, since it was tuberculosis vaccine, let her stick herself first, then she could stick me.

"You're the one that is the inmate," he said. Yeah, but I was not going to take the shot. "Then you have to go to lockdown," the deputy said.

I was willing to go to lockdown rather than take a needle with some unknown drug in it. They didn't put me in lockdown that time. I am sure people wondered why I was so paranoid about that shot. What was so strange about that shot is when they came to get me to arrest me the first time, we were getting ready for a Falcon preseason football game. Friends were expected at our home.

There were some strange activities in our community. There were some meth heads hanging around and nobody seemed to know why they were in such an exclusive neighborhood. Understand my family was the only black family in the entire community. My wife said she heard sounds as if someone was trying to get into our back door. I was in the shower getting ready for the football party. "Honey, somebody is trying to get in our door," Anita said. I said call the cops.

When the police came, they told us they found a woman and man roaming the neighborhood. Supposedly police talked with them on the curb. Police let them go. When police came, they asked my wife for me, and she asked them to step inside the house. So, we naturally thought they were there because someone was breaking into our home.

"John McNeil?" the officer asked.

"Yes," I answered boldly.

"We have a warrant for your arrest," the police said.

"Arrest for what?" I asked.

"For murder," the deputy answered.

"Murder who?" I asked puzzled.

"Brian Epp," the deputy said.

"Where is the detective? I was told if there had been any new evidence, any new investigation or anything new that came up, they would come here and tell me about it or call me to come to the station," I said angrily.

"He disapproved. He didn't come," the deputy responded. "Sir, turn around and put your hands behind your back."

The detectives who were there the day of the shooting refused to come with them to arrest me. They contended that there had not been a crime and did not want to be part of the arrest.

I thought something was wrong. Thankfully, my sons were not at home to see this. They were out with their friends. As they took me out to put me in back of the cruiser, there was a syringe with something in it lying on the floor of the car. My wife saw me hitting my head on the window of the car screaming, "Get me out of here."

My wife came running and I told her about the syringe lying on the floor. The deputies said they didn't know anything about it and that one of the meth heads must have dropped it inside the car. But the meth heads supposedly never got in the car. So, how did the needle get there?

The deputies took the needle and put it in a plastic baggie and put it in the trunk of the car. Remembering this, I had every reason to be suspicious of the needle the nurse was going to give me. Maybe there was really medicine in it as they said. Maybe there was something else in that needle. I was not going to trust them. They were not trustworthy.

Chapter 10: Georgia Diagnostics and Classification Prison

Once you have been found guilty, the prison administration puts you on a bus and takes you to a place they called the Georgia Diagnostics and Classification Prison. While there, inmates are classified and sent to another prison or choose to serve time there at that prison.

They take your fingerprints and your DNA, and they swab you to see if you have sexually transmitted diseases. They give you shots. I was told I could be held there for thirty days until they found a bed for me. I was going to a level five prison for inmates they have difficulty being in control of. The only level worse than five is level six—the most secure of the prisons. The Diagnostics Prison is level six.

When you hear people say being in jail is worse than being in prison, it means they have a misdemeanor charge, like shoplifting. Something small. For them the county jail is probably the worse they have seen because they only had to be in a short period of time. None of it is easy. There are levels of bitterness, with prison being the most bitter.

Prison is much rougher than jail. They try to scare you in the county jail, but it still is nothing like being inside of an actual prison, trust me. That seems to be why people are sent to prison, because it is so bad. I have heard people say, when they are angry or trying to make a point about how strongly they feel, that they would commit a crime and serve the time wearing a smile. I doubt that very much. It would not take long for the person to change their tune.

What makes prison so bad is the living conditions, such people of different cultures, the food, the climate, and the fact that you don't have freedom. I don't know about federal; I was only kept in state facilities.

When I think about Georgia, I think about the movie *Ray*. You know the song says that Georgia stays on my mind? I can never forget Georgia. I believe I was tagged by prison administration when I went into prison, and inmates knew that as well. There were beds running down both sides of the wall with one row of beds down the center, like it is in the military. There were individual showers and toilets.

There was a white guy with a bald head looking at me. He was in the Aryan Brotherhood. "We are familiar with who you are," he said to me. "You won't make it out of here alive." And from that, I didn't know where and/or what form of death would come for me. I knew they (the Epp family) wanted me dead. That guy walked away from me toward about fifteen other guys. I knew I could not confront him. He wanted to fight, and it would have been me against all of them. I knew I had to keep my wits and be smart as soon as I got inside. There was no time to rest. I had to figure things out quickly.

I went up to an older black guy and started talking to him. In prison you can't ask a lot of questions about anybody because it meant you're trying to put a hit on that person. It also meant they will try to come and get you first. You have to be careful inquiring about anyone. So my question was a general one. "How often do the officers come around here and check? Has anybody ever been killed inside the dormitory?" I asked him. The old black guy looked at me. His eyes were empty.

He finally spoke. "No, not to my knowledge," he said. "They have had a few stabbings."

I asked, "Inside here?" He said yes. "When did it take place? In daylight like around noon, or when it's dark when people go to sleep?" I wanted to know.

As I expected, he knew the answer. "Basically, when the guys lie down to get some rest, the guys will watch you doze off and stab you up." Now I knew it was not safe to sleep. I needed to figure out a way to get some rest.

I teamed up with a guy that I knew from Atlanta that I used to play ball with. I didn't really know him; I just remembered I played basketball against him a few times. I had to be careful what I asked. "You look familiar. I think I played basketball with you somewhere." That is how I began my conversation with him. I asked him if he was from Atlanta, and he said yes. I asked him which gyms he played in, and he named a gym I used to frequently played there. Thank God he remembered me from that gym.

Then I was clear to ask questions about some of the people in the dorm. "This is supposed to be an honor dorm, but they have more things going on in here and more people getting hurt in here than they do in the thunder dorm," he told me. I told him that I knew I was there by myself, and I asked him not to let them all jump on me. He said he had my back.

A day later he brought me back a shank, a prison knife. "What am I supposed to do with this?" I asked him.

"You'd better take it, because you never know when you might need it to get them off of you," he told me. "Or you might need it to keep them from getting on you."

And this was the honor dorm—not even the really bad dorm. I didn't know how I was assigned to the dorm I was in. Normally you had to be taking educational classes and have a work detail, but I had just gotten there. I guess it was just the grace of God. I didn't choose any classes when I went in there, so I didn't know why they treated me special. Maybe they could have known the NAACP was involved and my case was one to watch. I had to hide my shank in different places; under my mattress, under my sweatshirt, but never in one place for very long. You didn't want another inmate to find it and you didn't want an officer to find it. They came in every so often to shake your locker box down to make sure you didn't have anything illegal.

A locker box is what inmates call where they keep things.

There was nothing about prison that was good. From the minute you walked in the door, it was scary. I thank God that first guy didn't get me. They certainly could have, because we were in an open dorm. I stayed there until they shipped me to Smith State Prison.

The interesting thing about prison was that you got to watch everything around you. It was like your senses become super-sensitive and alert. Usually you were watching out for your life, but sometimes you got a chance to watch how people from outside of prison interacted with inmates.

The guys inside needed things, many things, from cigarettes to potato chips. When you are in prison, there are things that you need. Without someone to put money on your account, your life is far more problematic inside. You have nothing to bargain with. Many guys have families who no longer call, write or visit. That is hard.

Guys get illegal cell phones with internet capabilities. And guys meet women online.

Unfortunately, there are too many women who have low self-esteem and just want somebody to love them. They want that "I love him and he loves me." Inside, inmates work out a lot and look as if they really take care of themselves. When women came to visit, they thought they had hit the jackpot. Why would a woman take up a relationship with a man who's in prison? He knows she is vulnerable, and he tells her that he loves her. Well, she may think it is better than she can do outside. This is a strong masculine man with a six-pack. Women want to hear the man loves them and before you know it, she is putting money in his account. Some women even bring their girlfriends to meet other inmates, and in some cases these guys have several women who come to see them and put money in their accounts. After they get to know them, they even yell at them and degrade them if they are late on their day to visit. Can you imagine? He can't go anywhere, but he yells when she comes late. The women take it and allow the inmate to dominate them. I always felt bad when I saw women who didn't deserve that. All of those things made me love my wife more and admire her strength and wisdom.

Chapter 11: Is This It, Lord?

At Hancock State Prison there was a prison worker named Mrs. Ashanta Lewis. After I had been in that prison about thirty days in solitary confinement, around the thirty-first day the flap opened to the prison door.

The flap on the door of the prison cell is a lifeline. It is the only contact you have with another human being, and it is not total contact. You can't open it. It is available only to them. When you are in solitary, you wait for the flap to open.

This particular day Mrs. Lewis opened the flap. The cell was dark like midnight without the moon. She said, "McNeil, come to the window." My senses were on high alert. She was telling me, not asking me. But her voice didn't sound especially gruff or angry. I came to the window and didn't say anything to her.

"How are you doing?" she asked me.

I was angry. All I could think of was me being imprisoned and how the system failed me. My and my son's lives were threatened, but because I am African-American and I defended myself in my own backyard, I was stuck in a place that I would not wish on anyone. I was just what anyone would expect—angry. I knew it would not be to my advantage to tell her how I felt. What could she do about my sentence? What could she do about the fact that my wife had no idea what happened to me? So, I answered her question with a question. "How should I be doing?" I asked her.

She waited a second. I could hear her shift her feet outside my cell. "Is there anything you need?" she asked.

Sometimes in basketball when a person throws you the ball a little harder than they should, you will throw it back a little harder than they did. It becomes a test of strength. I knew they were testing my strength and my mind was strong, not weak. "I need a lot," I responded. "What is it that you are offering that you could possibly give to me here?" They were sharp and probing, but I chose my words carefully. She was the librarian.

"I can get you some books to read. It will be a couple of weeks before I can get back." Just for the heck of it, I asked for medical magazines and home interior magazines. The flap closed. I didn't ask for a Bible. I know I probably needed to read, but at that time I was relating to God and the God that was within me.

When I look back, I can see how God prepared me for the dreadfulness of prison. I would lie down, my face on the ground, praying. Some days I would be naked in prayer because I felt I wasn't making a connection. What a test... I was in solitary without anything to help me make a transition. There was nothing to prepare me for the evil that was to come. A week went by. I heard what Mrs. Lewis had said to me, but I knew nothing anyone said could be trusted.

There was nothing about this world I was in that even made me hope for a book to read. There was no need for me to believe that the same people who put me in here would, with the same hand, then help me. I did pray while I was in there. I did not believe someone from inside there would be helpful to me. I put a shield around my heart. I had to protect myself against believing in anybody. I had believed in the justice system all my life. I always tried to do what was right. Look at what happened.

Then they sent Dr. Williams by to ask what I needed. I asked to talk to my wife. Ten days passed and, as I expected, it was as if I had fallen into a black hole. The next time the doctor came, he said, "We'll ask the warden." The flap shut again.

Whenever you made a request, to call your family, or any small thing you might request, they would not open your flap. They would promise an answer to your question. You might hear them walk by your cell, and you would wait for an answer to your question. Then the footsteps stop. No answer. Not even an acknowledgment that you were waiting for an answer. It was punishment inside the punishment.

It was well past my forty-fifth day in solitary, maybe close to the fiftieth day. I asked the doctor if there was a problem about me calling my wife.

He said, "Oh, the warden wasn't in, but let me check on it." There was never an answer to my questions without a delay. They always had to ask someone and get back to me. As harsh as it was, it taught me patience.

We say that we believe in God, but when you are in the pit of hell you *must* believe in God or lose hope. So I would plug into my spiritual realm. I prayed and I meditated.

This meditation was a good thing for me. Before I went to prison, I was a great "Sunday church" person. I would ride up to the church in a luxury car. I wore designer suits and expensive jewelry. My family was dressed beautifully. I carried a nice big old

Bible. I looked the part. But I didn't have not one ounce of the Word of God in me. I just looked like I did.

When I think back, at the time I didn't understand it. Those six years went by at turtle speed. From day one until the day you get out of prison, you remember it all. You remember what you went through. There are no good days in prison. The only thing about prison that would make it a good day is that I could open my eyes. That meant God had not taken me yet. So that became the reason for the good day. I would open my eyes and begin by thanking God for allowing me to see another day.

I didn't know if I would live through the day, but I did live through the night. Some people tell me they get up every day and read *Our Daily Bread*. My daily bread was my talk with the Master of heaven and earth. "Lord, I thank you for today," I would say. "Lord, it is going to be an awesome day." And I was in the hell of prison, I would still say it was going to be a good day.

I couldn't walk anywhere, just back and forth in the cell. It would only take about five steps and I would be at the front of the cell. Turn around, five steps and I am at the back. In some cells you can see the swirl in the floor from where the inmate who was in the cell before you had walked back and forth and turned around, much like you see a tiger in a cage. When I have looked at those big tigers and lions in the cage, I have always felt sorry for them, but when you are in the pit of hell and all you can do is wait, and you are being tried on every hand, then your faith can work.

And in all of the awfulness of the prison, my health was not a problem the whole six years. No blood pressure, nothing. If I had blood pressure problems, they would not have known it, because they didn't check my blood pressure until I got out of solitary. When you are in solitary, any health problems can present themselves. You would just have to live with it or die. I lost fifty-five pounds in solitary. When I got out, some of the inmates thought I was sick.

That is how much weight I had lost. I had not seen myself in solitary because there is no mirror. There was only a toilet, a sink and a bed. You were unaware of what you looked like.

I thought about the book of Job a lot in prison. I understood it was quite a test. I know that God knew what was in my heart. I could not fool him. So, I cried out to him. I asked him "Is this it, Lord? Is this going to be it for me?" I wondered if that was where I would die. My sentence in prison was life, but I was talking about the cell I was in. Would that be my life? That is how disconnected I was.

I couldn't make a phone call. I couldn't receive any mail. I couldn't see anybody. It was like they had sent me into this place to die, literally. So all I could think of was what Job said: he came into the world naked and he would go out naked. I gave up to die. There was nothing left. I cried out day in and day out. I might as well have been fasting. They were not feeding me often. I went into a deep prayer. Then the hunger that I had I didn't think about. Things had changed from my first night in solitary. I went in and I was mad. I paced the floor and I screamed out loud. I kicked the door. I understood why children kick when they are angry. It is the only outlet you have. I wasn't trying to destroy or damage the door, I was trying to release the emotions, feelings and the harshness of being helpless. Consider this: I was put in prison and that was wrong. I was in solitary confinement and that was wrong. They wanted me to lose my mind. How much could any human stand? That was why I thought to ask the Lord if this was the end.

When they put me in solitary, it was very hot outside, which meant stifling inside. The cells were only about six feet by eight feet, not a lot of room. I am six feet four inches tall and I could stand in the middle of the floor and touch both walls.

In most homes, there is a lid over the toilet. There was no lid and not even a toilet seat in prison. There was only the bare rim to sit on. When someone in the cells next to you used the bathroom, you could smell it in your cell. Sometimes the guys had something they call a roll-up. It was when they rolled up some tobacco in toilet paper. The smell of that came in through the vents and it smelled nasty. And there was the smell of perspiration. There was no window to open. You just had to endure it.

Each person who is in solitary is supposed to be able to answer to the charges against them in thirty days. I was in there eighty days before they allowed me to go before the disciplinary court. They asked me if I was guilty, and I said no. Then they said, "This one is on us. The next time it is on you. Not guilty."

I still waited an additional ten days in solitary, because they said they didn't have a cell for me to go into population at Smith State Prison. Solitary confinement is meant to break a man's spirit and soul. If a person does not lose some of themselves locked up there, it means that person has relied on something other than themselves, for example, a higher power, to get them through.

I remember the first night I was in solitary confinement all I did was cry, cry and cry. It felt like my world had ended. The sorrow swallowed me up whole, like falling into the abyss—falling helplessly in darkness.

In some prisons, they say they give their people in solitary confinement an hour a day outside. This was not what happened in my case. I was in solitary confinement twenty-four hours a day, seven days a week. I could not tell if it was day or night. The little window was painted so I could not see the sun. I never got to smell fresh air. I was inside the whole time. There was no exercise. The only exercise was when I gathered the strength to do push-ups. Sometimes I would run in place.

Thirty days with no change of clothes. Thirty days without talking with my family or with anyone else. Thirty days with no human contact. Thirty days in a human box. Thirty days to drive you crazy. You can lose track of time.

If you have a mind to, you can count the days by the way they turn the lights on and off. The lights went out at midnight. They were back on at 5:30 a.m. During the hours from midnight until 5:30 a.m., it was pitch black. You couldn't see your hand in front of your face.

I thought of my wife. Anita did not know where I was. I thought about my mother. I thought about my sons.

While in the darkness, I thought of a song my grandmother taught me. I began to hum it in my mind. "Jesus loves me, this I know. For the Bible tells me so. Little ones to him belong. They are weak, but he is strong." From that song I would sing, "He's an on-time God. Yes, he is."

That is what sustained me. I was in the lion's den. I was in a dungeon. I was in the belly of the beast.

When I was not crying, I did everything I could do to keep myself sane. I didn't want to go insane, but did all this break me down? Yes, it did.

I was lying on my bunk and my eyes were tired from crying, but tears flowed nonstop like a river. I saw there was something written on the ceiling. I had to clear my eyes from the tears so I could read it.

I don't know why I was drawn to what was written up there. I guess it was because someone wrote it on the ceiling. "Don't let them get your mind. They already have your body." I thought about that. I said, "Thank you, Lord." He put it on somebody's heart to write it, and there it was for me.

When I look back now and all of the hard things, I was writing letters during the day. I know when Anita got my letters she probably could not read them because there were so many tears and the water would mess up the ink. I was just pouring my heart out to her.

Even though she was battling cancer, she was my pillar of strength. I didn't get any mail from her for ninety days. She knew something was wrong. She got on the phone and she called.

After thirty days, the counselor came by and asked if everything was all right. "North Carolina has been calling, and we told them you were in confinement because there was a misunderstanding," she said to me.

"First of all, you don't go to confinement on a misunderstanding," I said. I told both the counselor and the doctor—again—that I needed to call my wife.

"I'll try to get by to you next week," the doctor said.

There is never a sense of urgency. That is part of the way they control you. They know you are anxious. They know your family is anxious. But they can keep you away from your family. They know that hurts.

That week they promised turned into two weeks. It was a month before anyone actually came. Many times when someone would come by, they would open the flap and then shut it back quickly. However, they would write on your chart as if they had really taken the time to see you. That was for the officers to cover their behinds. You wonder about the officers who are there. You wonder what happened to them as humans that they didn't think prisoners are human. African-American officers did not look at us any different. I found there are two kinds of black people. There are those who have been taught and understand what is going on around them. Then there are those who have not been taught and are fearful of what may happen. That is true if the person is a prison guard or just a guy on the street. When you talk about those officers and civilians in Georgia, we are talking about the Deep South. And there is a difference between those who only lived in the South and those who have lived in the North. Down there, they call it "the dirty south." So, a lot of the blacks are afraid and will not help you or treat you as if you are human. When you encounter the guys from the North, they seemed to understand you can't keep your mouth shut or you might perish. I was raised in the South, but I had the northern attitude. So, you try to pair up with the northerners. And of course you can't help but run into some with the fearful attitude.

You could never trust them because they always go back and tell what they know.

The first thirty days, I was not given the opportunity to change my clothes. There were inmates on both sides of me. But there was no way to talk to each other. The walls were solid concrete.

You could scream through the wall, but the other person could not hear you enough to know what you were saying. Sometimes you could hear a thump on the wall. I could not hear them talking on either side of me.

Chapter 12: Hancock State Prison Muslims and Christians

I met a guy named Eddie Smith in Hancock State Prison. He was a short guy, no more than five foot six. Eddie wasn't a big guy, but he was muscular from doing push-ups and pull-ups. He had a life sentence for shooting a white guy in Atlanta. Eddie wanted me to read his transcripts. After doing some research, this guy was innocent.

They didn't have resources to fight in court, so he was in prison. He had been in about twenty-five years. Every time he came up for parole, they set him back for another five or eight years. Eddie was a Muslim. I don't believe he became a Muslim

when he was a free man, but I do believe he
became a Muslim inside prison. When people are in prison, they join a religion or organization so that they can be a part of
something bigger. If you don't join something, you could be violated. I saw a lot of
guys convert to Islam inside prison. Muslims protect each other. They believe they
are their brother's keeper. They wanted me
to be a Muslim. I could have made the
choice to become a Muslim. My upbringing
didn't allow that. I was a little boy about
six years old, and I was taken to Wilson
Chapel Church. Sally McNeil, my grandmother, was a member there. My grandmother had a friend named Mrs. Shipman.
Mrs. Shipman had a lot of grandchildren.
We came up in a time when we all were
learning about ourselves and who God was.
I think my early upbringing and learning
about God at such an early age made it impossible for me to be anything else other
than a Christian.

Eddie approached me. "Man, you are a
mild, quiet kind of guy. You may need this,"

Eddie said to me. I had been in three fights in prison. I am a quiet guy, but there are times when you have to put some bass in your voice. You can't be a nice guy all of the time. If you are, you will be tried every minute of the day.

Eddie wanted to introduce me to Islam. "John, have you ever read the Qur'an?" I told him no. "It's almost like the Bible, John. They have some of the readings from the Bible," Eddie told me. I didn't know that. "I'd like to read it with you sometimes," Eddie said.

I told him OK. I thought it might be interesting to get to know Eddie a little better. I wanted to see his thought process. I like knowing how others think. It helped me as a basketball player to win as I played around the globe, and in college and later in business by knowing how others processed things. It also helped me in prison.

So, I was applying the same rules I had way back then. I read the Qur'an with him. Then he invited me to Jumu'ah. That is held on Fridays, what in the Christian

church they would call a service. I thought
to myself, Cool. That was the first time I
had actually seen hundreds of Muslims together praying. I didn't pray with them, but
I was there inside the mosque. I was standing in the back. I was a guest and because I
was not a Muslim, I couldn't get down with
them and pray. You couldn't just walk in
and pray.

As I was watching them, I thought how
cool it was to see them all in unison get on
their knees, pray and then come back up. I
mean everybody all together gets right back
up.

I thought, How cool. There were all races:
black, white, Arab, Latino. They were all
praying together with one accord. I say the
white guys were Muslim for protection. But
as great as it was to observe, it was not for
me, because I am a Christian. I have respect for them. What I learned during my
time with them helps me to this day.

I even fasted during Ramadan. I fasted
with them for thirty days, sunup until sun-
down. Oh my God, the first two days were

horrible. That first week is especially hard. At 4 a.m. I got up and prayed before the sun came up in my dormitory. In the evening when the sun went down, I ate. I wanted to see how it felt. I wanted that cleansing. While they prayed to Allah, I prayed to my Jesus the Christ. It was the cleansing I was after. I wanted that special place with my Master. I got that during fasting and meditation.

During the month of Ramadan, the prison allowed Muslims to eat according to their belief in fasting. They made special provisions for them to eat before the sun came up and after the sun went down.

I began to mingle with them and talked with them so much that people thought I was a Muslim. They greeted me "As-Salaam-Alaikum." And I would return, "Wa-Alaikum-Salaam."

When they read the Qur'an, I read it with them. Then I would go to my cell and read my Bible. When you don't know something, it makes you respond differently. When I was a kid my mom would put something on my plate I did not know. I would immediately tell her I did not like it. She would ask if I had ever had it, and I would say no. She would ask how I knew I didn't like it. I said, "It didn't *look* like I should like it!" It is the same thing with life. How was I to know about Islam unless I put myself in the path to know? Experiences are the best teachers. If I had never gone to Jumu'ah, I would have never known how they prayed. It wasn't that I was trying to be one of them, but now I understand them. I count it a gift to have had that time with them.

Attending Jumu'ah made me think of Malcolm X, who was converted to Islam in prison. They called him Red before he went to prison and then he transformed in prison to Malcolm X. I went to prison as John. I came out as John McNeil. That is what the world knows me by now, John McNeil. I compared our lives. I thought, Malcolm was a Muslim and he was transformed through the prison system. Now, here I was in prison and I also did a lot of spiritual transforming

when I came out. Whatever God's purpose
is for your life, that is the path he will have
you on. I could have easily become a Muslim, if that is what God had wanted me to
be. In my heart of heart and in my spirit, I
am a Christian.

John was that young Wilson County guy
who ran around playing basketball and who
was a basketball star around these parts of
Wilson County. They knew me as John, the
businessman in Atlanta. I was still a young
man in my thirties. When I went to prison,
I was almost forty years old. I got out and
came back to Wilson and people remembered the young John. But this John is ma-
tured both spiritually and secularly. I am a
middle-aged man who went through a
storm, who lived in the lion's den, who sur-
vived the dungeon. It is John McNeil they
don't really know. John and John McNeil
are different. Young John is gone.

When I attended Jumu'ah, I would listen. The lessons were familiar in some
ways, yet unfamiliar. They would bring
from a Muslim perspective what they be-

lieved Allah was saying. Their speakers were so elegant. If you were to have asked me before I was in prison if I thought an incarcerated man could speak so flawlessly, so elegantly, so brilliantly, I would have said no. A variety of Christian churches would come in to have services with us. And although I am Christian and they are Christian, the messages they gave were not like what I was getting from the Muslims, so it would have been so easy for me to be persuaded to be a Muslim. The thing about the Christian churches is that while I believe some were sincere, they put themselves on a pedestal. They were the good church people coming to help us, the poor old sinful inmates locked up. As well meaning as some of them were, they came with a message and they wanted us to hear that message. They thought of us as guilty people who were paying on earth for our sins. They did not come with an ear to hear what might be happening to us. They didn't see what the conditions were, nor did they ask. They came to tell us Jesus loved us, but they didn't really understand that message themselves.

I found a spiritual connection in common with the Muslims although we were in different faiths. Sometimes we have tunnel vision. It is so easy to say, "If you are not over here with me, then you are wrong."

There is a sermon I remember from a Pastor Wilson. He said even when we think what we are doing is right, on the other side it may seem to be wrong.

Some people may think that I was wrong as a Christian to worship with Muslims. But I believe God had me go over there. I can't say why God had me go over there with them, but I knew it was different. There was a spirituality over there that was different from what I was used to. Before prison I had been invited to mosques, and I always politely turned down the invitation.

I knew about humility in prison. Before I went to prison, I heard someone say we are one breath away from death and one paycheck away from being homeless. In prison I learned what that meant. I learned I was just a breath away from death. When you are making five-figure bonuses, you don't consider those things because you don't have to. When I was prosperous, I didn't think about anything like that. In times past, I never depended on anybody. I could do it all myself, so I thought. It is a humbling situation. The words fail me to say what it feels like at this particular time, at this particular point and in this particular situation.

Eddie, who invited me to come to Jumu'ah, didn't think I would take him up on his offer to go to worship with him. He was one of my first workout partners at Hancock State Prison. We would do ten sets of pull-ups and then chin-ups. We could do a thousand push-ups within an hour. I had a six-pack back then. We did lunges and squats.

Eddie used to tell me that the mind was ready to go, but we had to get the body ready as well. He used to say over and over, "I'm getting you ready to go home." He was

getting me ready for my path. He was telling me my future and I thought to myself,
Do Muslims believe as Christians about
prophecy?

When he would say that I had to prepare
myself to go home, I wondered what he
knew that I didn't know. I was only two
years into my sentence, and I knew my goal
was to go home, but I didn't know what all
had to take place before I was released from
prison. I would serve another four more
years.

Many times, as Christians, we think we
have arrived and we should not interact
with Muslims or Buddhists because they
are not connected with God. We should only
mingle with other Christians. But I have
come to know in my heart that there is only
one God. No matter what your religious belief is, or whatever your preference is, there
is only one God. Christians believe that God
used a donkey. Well then, he certainly can
use us. He can use a Muslim.

Chapter 13: What About Me

When I think about my time in prison and think about those people in the bible who went through so much, I know it was predestined for me to go through prison. Notice, *through* prison. Not around it, but through it. I think by my journey somebody else was touched. I believe through my testimony somebody else was delivered. Somebody else was healed—male and female.

I don't think it happened at the outset. But they got to see my situation through the media's eyes. They got to read about my story in the newspapers. They heard about it on radio. And lo and behold, to the glory of God, they saw the man that God brought out.

Many people may have their opinion of prison and have no feelings for inmates. But I would not wish prison on my worst enemy. I would never wish it on their family. People don't consider what effect prison has on their family: it destroys them. Yes, there are some who are in prison who have done wrong by society's standards. They get to have that "time out." And yes, a lot of people in prison say they are innocent when they are not.

But I am here to tell you, there are many people who are inside the wall who are innocent, and it is a matter of race and/or poverty that keeps them in there. Lady Justice has a blindfold on and supposedly is only interested in what is right. But we have those who are looking, and they know if you are poor—black, white or Latino— your chance of getting a fair trial is next to impossible.

What would be interesting is if racism was put aside and those who are without power got together against those who keep us apart. The power shift would change.

Imagine not worshipping those who have millions and billions of dollars.

While racism has been around for thousands of years, the most devastating form of racism has been Western culture's racism toward people of color and, in particular, the institution of slavery. The power structure wants us all to fight each other. It is working. Poor whites hate poor blacks, and we are all in the same boat. Many poor whites believe the one advantage they have is that at least they are not black. Imagine what would happen if that kind of thinking was put aside and poor whites, poor blacks, Latinos and others whose necks have been stepped on by the system were seen as equals and entitled to equal justice.

Should I mention there are blacks who hate whites? Yes, there are. So let's get into the meaning of racism. Unfortunately, many use the word and don't know the meaning. Even some dictionaries have it wrong. A racist is part of a power group. Prejudice—to prejudge or favor—can be towards any person, no matter what the race.

Are black people able to keep anyone from housing, education, employment or the fair distribution of privilege? The answer is no. African-Americans are not a part of the power structure of this country in any form. So, poor whites, who have no power, are part of the power group. They may not personally control things, but their group does.

African-Americans can be prejudiced, but not racist. Let's look at the George Zimmerman case, where he shot and killed a teenager, Trayvon Martin. Zimmerman was praised by the National Rifle Association (NRA), and they rushed to help and defend him without his asking for it. Zimmerman put himself in a situation where he was in a confrontation with Trayvon. In my case, I was in a state where there are **STAND YOUR GROUND** laws. The NRA is passionate about **STAND YOUR GROUND** laws. The city I was living in had particularly intense laws that said every head of household must have a firearm and bullets for the gun. In my case, my son was threatened and I was confronted in my own yard. Unlike Zimmerman, I was thrust into a confrontational situation. But there was silence in support of me. My support came from the NAACP and my hometown. After all, the **STAND YOUR GROUND** laws don't seem to be for African-American men who protect their families. So, if the poor and powerless were to act with one accord, it would be the beginning of positive change in this country. It amazes me that a rich person can lie and steal, and society will reward that person with giving them millions more. We saw that with the great recession and the great financial crisis of 2007–2008.

A poor person can take some food and to prison they will go. A well-to-do man's son can rape someone and never be charged. Even the girl who is raped and her family will keep silent out of fear that the man's family is connected somehow to power. A poor man's son will do time and be innocent of the crime. Those who are outside of prison should care about what happens inside of prison. The people inside should not be discarded like trash. There are redeemable souls there. There are innocent people there. There are those whose lives will never be turned around in there. If I could give any advice, I would ask each governor and each state's attorney general, along with district attorneys, to look into the justice system.

Are those who prosecute interested only in how many people they succeed at locking up, or are they interested in justice? Politics overrides and destroys lives and families. Prosecutors too often appear to be interested in saying how many wins they have. Winning helps local prosecutors to be promoted to federal prosecutors. They use their wins to get promoted. Nobody counts to see how many were wrongfully imprisoned. There should be police review boards made up of citizens who look into how police carry out their duties. Are prosecutors and police only looking for low-hanging fruit, the easily convicted? Or are they looking to improve our justice system?

I have to interject and say that the police who testified for me were interested in justice. They went against the grain and did what was right. Many never would have done that. I will always be grateful. I just want to say I know that all officers are not bad. There are good people on the force, and I know many of them. But the system overall needs revision.

If I could meet with the President, I would tell him an executive order is needed to look into the prison system. State legislators need to put committees together who would have the task of going to the different counties, going into the prisons and doing interviews to find out what is going on.

It would be great for them to see how African-American men are being put in prison when some don't need to be there. The system says the men broke the law. If you go back and look, you can see where something was stacked against them, and most of them pled guilty because they were uneducated. They didn't know the law. They didn't really understand their rights. What you don't know can kill you.

When I got into prison, I began learning how to read the transcripts and look at cases. I began doing paralegal work. I started looking at my own case. I have to admit, when I was going through the court system, I didn't know what they were talking about. We were paying lots of money and I was sitting in court and they were all talking in a language I didn't understand. Only the attorney, the judge and the district attorney really understood what was being said, bargained and concluded. You see people on trial looking like they don't know what is being done. It is because they don't know. You sit there as a defendant and you think your attorney has your best interest at heart. At least that is what I thought. When it all concluded, I was headed to prison. While in prison, I began to read my transcript. I began looking at the laws that pertained to me. It caused me to ask questions that I would have thought the attorney would have asked. I would ask my lawyer questions and he would give me the same old story, but it didn't jibe with what the law was and what happened to me. When I would call and ask even more questions, he would say "Uh, let me check into that." He would never get back to me. My case was over. He was on to the next person.

I know now you don't trust your life into someone else's hands. You put your life in the hands of the one you can trust, the one who deserves your respect, and that is God. Put your life in God's hands.

There is a school-to-prison pipeline. There are people who go around and talk about the importance of stopping the intense punishment of African-American children in school, but we aren't accomplishing what we set out to do. Sometimes there are partial victories, and then we sit down.

Chapter 14: My Dream Deferred

I was able to smile in court that day, February 12, 2013, when I knew I was coming home to North Carolina. I even laughed on the inside. Here I am pleading guilty to voluntary manslaughter, a crime a jury found me not guilty of.

Some people still think I should have stayed in prison rather than saying I was guilty of voluntary manslaughter. It is easy for people to theorize about what I should have done. I had just lost Anita. I knew I was not going to be able to hold her in my arms. She was gone forever on earth. I wanted to at least be there for her burial. I had missed my mother's funeral because I wasn't allowed to be escorted by the local law enforcement here in Wilson, and Anita wanted me to come home. "John, you can fight for yourself better out here than inside. You can meet different people. You can get things done. You know what it is going to take to get you totally free. Somebody else may speak on your behalf, but they won't completely know what you know," Anita told me.

I know she was right. Learning the law myself as a layman and how it applied to me was extremely helpful. As a prisoner, I had to fill out a form to be able to go to the law library. Although there was a general library where you go to read books and magazines, the law library was a different section. There were three sessions for going to the law library. There was a morning, afternoon and evening session. There would be at least ten guys in the library. The guys who frequented the law library had hope they could work on their case and get freedom. Many of them had been banged around, but they still had faith in the law. They also began to help other inmates who didn't know anything about the law. They became self-made lawyers. Some guys had turned their knowledge of the law into a hustle. Inmates would pay other inmates to do law work for them. There were some prison lawyers who were really good. Some had not been successful in getting themselves out but were successful in getting other inmates out. They had written their own briefs that lawyers took to court.

I became a law library clerk. And in that time, I began to help others as well. I wrote some briefs and some motions. I wrote some of my own briefs and sent them to my lawyer I was paying. They used some of my research to defend me. They told me my work was good. It needed some fine-tuning but was usable. I had nothing but time to do research. I could spend my time doing nothing, or I could spend my time defending myself. Being right there at the law library and having lots of time meant doing work on my own case.

When you research cases, you look for lawsuits that are similar to your own. There were no cases like mine. I began looking at the cases of Strickland v. Washington and Brady vs. Maryland. I knew I had a Brady violation; they said I did at the habeas corpus court, even though in the next breath Judge George took it away and said no.

Brady v. Maryland is a landmark U.S. Supreme Court case where prosecutors were said to have withheld evidence from the defense. Brady and his companion Boblit were charged with murder. Brady admitted being involved, saying Boblit actually killed the person. Documents stated that the prosecution held back a statement that Boblit actually confessed to being the person who did the killing alone. The defendant challenged his conviction, stating it violated due process, and the U.S. Supreme Court agreed.

The Brady case talked about withholding evidence from the defense, and in my case they did just that. The prosecutors lied and

said that Epp's drug test came back nega-
tive and that he was never a felon. They
held that information from me. In fact, he
was on methamphetamines the day he at-
tacked my son, and he was in fact a felon.
The Brady v. Maryland case speaks to that
fact. But the assistant prosecutor said he
had no knowledge of it. How could he not
know, as he was just a town away from
where the man was convicted? The same
things applied to my attorney. How could
they not know this? All of the attorneys had
to have known. Private investigators let my
new lawyer know of the drugs in Epp's system and his felon conviction. Mind you, I
never had any run-ins with law enforcement. I was not a drug user. I was a law-
abiding citizen.

I knew there was something strange
about this guy. The reason I say that is because I have never seen anyone who was
willing to challenge someone with a gun.
He was the aggressor. What man in his
right mind would do that? I know I
wouldn't do that. Even if I were arguing

with someone and saw that they had a gun, my first instinct would be, I'm gone. I would never have done what he did. He kept challenging me and walking towards me. I fired the gun into the ground. He kept coming. So either the person is out of his mind, or he is high. He was high. The district attorney's office withheld the evidence, and that was clear. He was high!

Chapter 15: Getting Help Outside

When you are behind prison walls, it is difficult to know what is really going on outside on your behalf. Inside there is the same day-to-day struggle to stay alive. You hear from your lawyer and your family. One minute there is good news; the next minute there is bad news. There are always ups and downs.

I met Rev. William Barber, president of the North Carolina State Conference of the NAACP, through my wife, Anita, and family friend Frank Jones. Frank Jones is a member of the local Wilson Chapter of the NAACP. Anita and Frank took my case to

Rev. Barber to take a look at it in Goldsboro, North Carolina. But in order for the state NAACP to look at it, a letter had to be written by Anita and Frank to the local chapter. They had to agree to look into it and take it to the state. I was thinking, What is next?

We had just gone to the courts in Cobb County, and the motion was denied. The same lawyer who was my trial lawyer, Tony Axam, was working on the brief to go to the Georgia State Supreme Court.

It didn't take long to get the North Carolina NAACP involved. They said they also wanted the Georgia NAACP to look into the case. My case was very unusual, as the lead detectives and all the witnesses were on my side. When you get a detective with over twenty years of experience to go up against the district attorney, then that's really an unusual case. Something is definitely wrong.

My case was so strong that the NAACP took it to the national stage in New York. They took it as a resolution (34:02), and then this case got national attention. I was happy to know that people all over the country would know about what happened.

Another inmate saw a banner of me with my picture and a crowd of people on television. I didn't know that was happening. I was working out in the yard, and, sure enough, I ran into the dormitory, and on the television I saw them protesting in Cobb County. There was the Rev. William Barber, the NAACP North Carolina State Conference president, Benjamin Jealous, the national NAACP president, Dr. Niaz Kasravi, then director of the NAACP's Criminal Justice Program, and Edward DuBose, the NAACP Georgia State Conference president. There were so many people that supported my cause. I thank God for working through these people.

Other inmates were not happy for me. In contrast, they were angry with me. Unfortunately, so many blacks have learned self-hatred. Then there's Willie Lynch Syndrome, stemming from the eighteenth-century idea of setting slaves against each other in order to control them, manifesting as a modern-day lack of empathy for each other. Particularly in prison, Anita used to call me to tell me where they had been, and who they had been talking to. They were in Nevada and Washington, D.C. I knew it had become a movement. I had been lied to many times, but I knew Anita would never lie to me. I knew she would tell me the truth no matter what. Even though my sentence was life, I knew she would not leave me for another man. In life, God may give you your soul mate early or late. I didn't know at the outset that she was my soul mate, but through all of our trials and tribulations before this prison incident, I knew she respected what God had put in place for a husband and wife.

Anita was like the woman in Proverbs 31, the virtuous woman. Not one moment did I doubt her or think that she would turn her back on me. At no time did I doubt her in my heart and think she would run around on me. She was not that kind of lady, because I tested her spirit and I've known her since she was a young woman. There was not one time that I worried about Anita's devotion to me while I was in prison.

My worry for Anita was that something tragic would happen to her. She didn't have fear, and you don't see that too often. She believed, and she got me to believe to understand what a real relationship was. It meant to be truly committed in unity. She was my hero. I learned from her. It wasn't so much what she said but what she did and how she lived. She was a phenomenal lady.

I think about her and I can see her face. I think about when she came to Cobb County the first time to see me. Her heart was broken. I had made her a promise. I told her I would never hurt her. Then to see her there in prison, and to know that I could not keep that promise, it killed me inside. For generations, our forefathers were separated from their families and loved ones by slavery. People would love each other, and their masters had no feelings for them. They would sell one of the spouses, leaving the other to die on the inside.

That is the reason I go out and try to help the children in our community. I know that financially I am in bad shape, but you can't just think about yourself, you have to think about the people in your community. I know that I am not in this struggle by myself. It makes you appreciate your fellow man and know we can help each other.

After I was out of prison, I remembered a minister once saying that God did it for you, and you are like that old Timex watch commercial: "You take a licking and keep on ticking." You can't crumble every time you get a bump or bruise.

When I look back on all the times in prison when I was right there at death and danger, I could have lost my mind. I had death threats in prison and after I got out of prison. At that time, it seemed like God didn't let me see all of the danger that I was in, but now that I'm free, I know that it was right in my face, but I don't live in fear.

Chapter 16: They Want to Break Me

Before I begin talking about the hole, the prison within the prison, let me list the institutions I was in as a prisoner. I was in Baldwin for diagnostics; the second prison was Smith. When I left Smith, I went to Hancock. Then I was sent back to Baldwin. From Baldwin I went to Macon State. From Macon State, I was released to come back to North Carolina.

I was put in solitary at least three times while in prison. It wasn't because I had done anything wrong, but the prison officials were trying to break me. After the first time, it didn't have the same effect on me. The first time I was devastated. There was no need for them to think it would continue to have the same effect as the first time.

When they put me in solitary the next time, my mind was equipped for it. I didn't realize it the first time, but God was strengthening me. In order for you to get what God has for you, he has to decrease you. Then he comes back and increases you.

To understand what I am saying, if you plant one grain of corn, it will die first. But when it grows, it is better than it was when you put that one grain in the ground. More than one ear of corn will come on the stalk from that one grain of corn.

Nobody wants to go through the hard knocks, but it is the only way to grow. Who would want to go through prison? Nobody in their right mind would want that. But I did go through hard times and I did learn and grow from it.

The second time they threw me in the hole, they said I had an illegal cell phone. They did a search and didn't find anything, but they threw me in the hole anyway. Prisons are governed by the people who are outside. There was a lot of attention being brought to my case. There were marches in Cobb County, Georgia, with banners and all. Media was asking questions. People who heard about my case were asking how a man in a **STAND YOUR GROUND** state could be in prison for protecting his home. Any time there was publicity and lots of attention, they would start messing with me inside. As an inmate, I wanted people to know what was going on. I needed the publicity. But the more attention outside, the more punishment inside. So prison officials threw me back in the hole. They tried everything. They put me in a dorm with all gang members. Eight guys robbed me. It was a rough ride for me. The second time they put me in the hole, for supposedly having a cell phone, they put me in for sixty days. I was in Hancock and actually working for Mrs. Ashanta Lewis, the librarian. She came to see about me, but I could not trust any of the people there. I told her I was all right. I was thinking, Why am I in the hole? They know I didn't have anything. They said they were putting me in there on PI (pending investigation). That was bogus. The prison guards were trying to break me.

This particular cell was grayish and dark and dingy looking. They all pretty much had the same smell. There was no circulation in the air. This cell had more graffiti on the walls. Gang members put their gang signs on the walls.

This time, I took it like a champ. No crying. I did pray, but no tears. This time it was a workout facility for me. There was nothing but time, so I began doing my push-ups. I would walk in place, and I would do lunges and squats. It helped burn off stress and get rid of that extra energy. When you are confined like that, you still have that energy. You burn it off so you can relax. If I didn't work out, I would have been tense from thinking.

Since I have been to prison, I wear no jewelry. None. I haven't worn jewelry since I've been home. It is a transitional thing for me right now. Before prison I wore a Rolex and a diamond pinky ring and a wedding band. I won't say I won't ever wear jewelry, but not right now. Who knows, maybe a watch will be all. Only time will tell.

I never slept in the hole for any long length of time. I took catnaps. I would lie down and before long I would be back up. Not much time had passed. There was no way of telling time, but I counted the days by marking on the wall while I waited.

When I was there, Mrs. Lewis knew I had not done anything wrong. She was a young lady in her early twenties. Her mother was some kind of commissioner in Sparta, Georgia. Mrs. Lewis did have a heart. I used to talk with her. Her mother raised her in church. The good in her responded to the good in me. I think she was concerned about me. I think she helped to push to get me out of the hole in sixty days. I believe they would have kept me longer than that.

It is illegal to have a cell phone in prison. Understand, I didn't have an outside work detail. I wasn't allowed anywhere outside of the prison. Where would I get a cell phone from? If there were any cell phones, they would come from someone who had access coming and going from outside to inside. The only people who had access to going outside were guards and administrators. When I was released from the hole, I found that I was not guilty of having a cell phone.

The third time I went into the hole was when my case was overturned, and I was at Baldwin again. They put me in the hole again for an illegal cell phone that never existed. Then they dropped all of the disciplinary reports and transferred me in the middle of the night to Macon State Prison. It was 2:30 in the morning. I was by myself, shackled down—the scariest moment in my life.

There was a white officer named Jones and a black officer named Howard. It was the most alarming transfer I had ever had. I thought they had orders to kill me. I thought that was the whole purpose of transporting me. We did not go to Macon State Prison at first. We were in the back of an abandoned school. The grass was about five feet high. Everything was dark and quiet. I didn't know if they were just trying to scare me, but I believe they were going to kill me.

Then they stopped suddenly. I began to feel the hair rise on my arms and my neck. I knew something was not right. I was looking at the officers and they were looking at each other. Howard had a prepaid cell phone, like the illegal ones they sell to inmates in prison. I noticed both had regular cell phones on their belts. So, I wondered, why did he have a prepaid cell phone as well?

Howard, who was sitting on the passenger side, got out of the van. In the high weeds he began to walk to the back of the van. My heart began to beat real fast. I thought this was the last moment. I would be killed here and left in these weeds. Who would know what happened to me? I could hear my heart beating loud in my head.

Before I left to be transferred, I gave a guy Frank Jones's number and told him to tell Frank to let Anita know I was being transferred in the middle of the night. I asked him to call right away. It was an open dorm, so I talked to a second inmate.

The inmate looked fearful for me. "Man, I have never known them to transport somebody like this in the middle of the night," he said. "Man, something is wrong." Normally they would wait until daylight. I felt as if this was my last ride. We drove away and a million thoughts went off in my mind. Each and every moment I felt as if death was around each corner in prison. I always breathed a sigh of relief when I passed through a hairy moment. I didn't know what would happen this time. We were riding down the highway at a normal speed and then we turned off the road. That is also unusual.

When they stopped in back of the school, my heart dropped. I said to myself, this is it. I am about to die. As Howard walked to the back of the van where I was, I began to shake. I felt like I would pee on myself. I knew there was no way I could escape. I didn't know what to think. He came to the side and it looked like he was going to turn the handle and tell me to get out. But something happened. His phone rang again. He picked the phone up and walked away from the door. He stood there about five minutes. Then he got back in on the passenger's side. He and Johnson, the white officer, began talking, but I could not hear what they were saying.

They pulled off and rode around for another five minutes. I thought, Maybe they got the word not to kill me. Maybe the other prison wasn't ready for me yet. That would be no reason to go to an abandoned building. This is a game and I don't know the rules. But they went to another place that had high grass. Howard got out the van again. I was thinking, It is over. That was the wrong place. They had to move to another location.

My thoughts were like a thousand firecrackers had been tied together and were going off in my head. Pop, pop! Did that guy call Frank? Pop, Pop! What is Anita doing? Pop, pop. Who can I call to tell them I am in trouble to help me? Pop, pop. Who ordered me to be killed? Pop, pop. Is he going to shoot me in the head? Pop, pop. Will I die instantly? Pop, pop, pop. This time I am going to die. I said to myself, They are supposed to leave my body at a different location. They were never supposed to leave the highway with a prisoner. When my family asks, they will say I tried to escape. I was praying, "Lord, I need your help. I don't want to die right now, Lord. Help me."

When the officers put me in the van, they didn't search me. This time I *did* have an illegal cell phone on me. It was tucked away in the front of my pants. I took the chance to wiggle around and get that phone out. I called Anita. "Anita! Anita!" I was whispering because I didn't want the guards to hear me. I know I sounded funny.

"What's wrong, John?" Anita said sounding like she was waking up.

"They are transferring me to Macon State Prison right now," I told her.

She was wide awake now. "What? At three o'clock in the morning?"

"I think they are going to kill me," I told her. "I am in the back of some abandoned school. I know they are going to kill me."

"Hang up. I'm going to call for help," Anita told me.

I didn't know who Anita would call or what she would say. I knew I needed some help.

Howard's phone rang again. He talked for a few minutes and then he turned around. Howard got back in the van again. They looked at each other. Johnson shook his head. This time I saw we were getting back on the interstate. I did get to Macon State. It was the most terrifying ride of my life. I still believe they were going to kill me. I believe whoever was on the call told them not to. I made it to Macon, which turned out to be the roughest prison I had ever been in.

Interview with Dr. Niaz Kasravi

Dr. Kasravi met Mr. John McNeil when she was asked by the NAACP national office to help with the campaign to get him released from prison. At the time of this case, Dr. Kasravi was the director of the NAACP's Criminal Justice Program. Her role was to work with different parties (state and national offices, and attorneys) to help coordinate support for John McNeil.

Dr. Kasravi believed that Mr. McNeil was found guilty of murder because of the double standard and differential treatment of minorities in this country. The data shows that, on average, minorities, especially African-

Americans, are less likely to be seen as justified in their actions as white Americans, resulting in systematic discrimination. Also, the sentencing likely would have been different if Mr. McNeil had been a white American, although the outcome also depended on which party had the resources for a better legal team.

Now, if both parties had been African-American, again, the outcome likely would have depended on the resources of the legal team. It is believed and seen time and time again that African-American lives are not viewed as equal to those of white Americans, and this occurrence might have been seen as another instance of black-on-black crime.

Although the NAACP and others were fighting for Mr. McNeil's freedom, his wife, Anita was instrumental and adamant about her husband's freedom. She was devoted to him and his case.

When asked if she would have still participated in the campaign to free John McNeil if she have not been paid, Dr. Kasravi stated,

"In addition to the fact that it was my job, absolutely, yes, I would have!"

Dr. Kasravi is currently founder and director of the Avalan Institute for Applied Research.

—Dr. Niaz Kasravi, interviewed by Tamara Chandler

Chapter 17: The Fight Going on Outside

From Frank Jones's Perspective

The NAACP was probably the vehicle that started the process of trying to get John out with any success. It all started with the local branch. John's mother and his wife were how I first heard of the trouble John had. When they called me and told me John had been arrested for murder, I almost fainted. I could not believe he had been charged with something so serious. Immediately I began to investigate what really took place. I made trips to Georgia. I went to see John in the Cobb County jail. I got a chance to talk to him and find out his side of what happened.

The way the jail is set up, you see the person, but you have to talk to them over a phone. It was a joy to see John come out the door. But to see him walk away, that broke my heart each time. It broke me up each time inside. The problem was to see them come and get him and he disappeared behind those doors. That will be with me for the rest of my life. I still get chills when I think about how that door would slam and I had to get up, walk out and leave him.

In that first meeting, I began to hear from John what happened. I knew his love for his family. I could not understand how anybody could treat such a good man so shamefully. So the next thing we had to talk about was what steps to take and what attorney to call. We wanted someone who we thought had a good shot at gaining John's freedom.

John first went to jail on August 11, 2006. There was no attorney. A few days later we were referred to Tony Axam by my sister. He was said to be one of the better lawyers in Atlanta. We heard he was a professor at Duke. He had the reputation for really working for his clients and looking for justice. Axam came to the jail immediately. John was traumatized by the whole thing. John stayed in jail until September 9, 2006. Because it was a murder case, John had to go before a judge.

Looking back, there are some questions I would have liked to ask Tony Axam about how he handled the case. I didn't know at the time, but I see it now. I think we should have brought up the lack of black males in the jury pool. Not one black male in the pool. That was the problem. It says a lot about the criminal justice system in Georgia that there would not even be a black man available.

Here's the thing I regret to today—I wish we had an attorney when I first came to see John. I believe it could have made a difference. He was charged nine months after the incident. I don't know what was on the minds of those people. I don't know if they felt as if John would just lie down, take this and not challenge them.

My first move, before I got back to Wilson, was to call my buddy, Rev. Barber. I was telling him I have a problem that needs to be investigated. We were just coming out of the James Johnson case, where a young man was accused of murder and sat in jail for years before he was released.

I think it helped John that the team was right in step with the process at that time. We had not cooled off from the James Johnson case. We just transitioned to the next battle. It was two separate cases, but the process was the same.

I took Anita to Goldsboro and we talked to Rev. Barber. The NAACP's process was that first it had to go through the local chapter. So, I went through the local branch. Alonzo Braggs was the president. The branch accepted the charge to try to assist John. Then the Georgia State Conference of the NAACP took it to the National NAACP. It was not a quick process. From the time we introduced the case, it took about a year and a half before we started making any progress.

Edward DuBose and Deane Bonner, Cobb County NAACP president, at first were not involved. That was so amazing because it happened in Georgia. You could throw a rock from the Cobb County jail to where the NAACP's office was, figuratively speaking. But they did not get involved. North Carolina got involved first. They heard about it in Georgia because there were so many news stories about it. I had been trying to reach out to Edward DuBose, but no results. When I would call, he would say he would get back with me. It was not a smooth process in the beginning, because I don't think he saw the urgency. Edward DuBose turned out to be one of the greatest fighters in this case. He still is fighting for John.

Believe it or not, we were in Kansas City, Missouri, for the state conference. I was on my way from the convention center to the hotel when I saw him again. Right there, Edward DuBose and I had a lengthy discussion. There we were: me, my wife, Bobbie, and Anita, along with Edward DuBose.

We met Edward DuBose in the crosswalk that connected the two hotels where the NAACP members were staying. That was where I think Edward DuBose bought into it. I would not let him get away from us again. I was determined to get to him to hear us out.

It was odd that the national president of the NAACP was not aware of John's case, being that John was in jail. The problem was trying to convince people what really happened. Most people were saying something had to have happened for him to be in prison. There was a presumption of guilt.

Rev. Barber and I went on the Mark Thompson Show in Kansas City, Missouri. Being on that show pulled the national NAACP's and others' coattails. By that time everyone realized we were not going anyplace. Rev. Barber and I were determined we were going to stay with them and keep John's case in front of them.

So, we had Edward DuBose's attention. Dr. Niaz Kasravi and Robert Rooks were in charge of the national NAACP's criminal justice arm. Rev. Barber was having some kind of criminal justice seminar in Williamston, North Carolina, in a small church. It was out in the cornfields.

Dr. Niaz and I became very good friends. We were in Williamston, North Carolina. The national director and Niaz came to Williamston and I met them at some second-rate hotel. I sat with them and sold them on the need for the national NAACP to be involved. I had statements. I had the overall picture of what happened in the trial. Dr. Niaz understood the criminal justice system and it wasn't hard to sell her.

The national branch wanted the NRA to be involved in this case. Here we are fighting like hell, and if the NRA had been interested in John's case, they should have come forward on their own to say something.

Former Congressman and federal prosecutor Bob Barr from Georgia made some overtones about going to the NRA. I could see them taking our efforts and using them against us in trying to get us to support the NRA in the future. There was no way we were going to allow the NRA to use us in that fashion. I did not want it to look like we were in bed with the NRA. I just didn't think that was the proper way to go. It may have been the way to go. I felt as if Chief Justice Sears, who looked at the case and said it was a miscarriage of justice, was who we should lean on. Not the NRA. She wrote the dissent and it was powerful. The dissent she wrote turned the eyes of many people.

Now the attorney general for the state of Georgia was a guy from Rocky Mount, North Carolina, by the name of Thurbert Baker. I faxed him all the necessary information, which I knew he already had. Baker could have made a difference, being he was a black, but he totally ignored us. I expected him to at least look at the information. That was one of the first setbacks we had.

I thought he would have connected with us, being he was African-American. I remember faxing the material to his office and I called. When the secretary answered,

I didn't say what it was, and she said it was coming through right then. It was information the NAACP had found in our investigation. It was totally ignored. He never said a word to this day. But now, how does one get to be black and the attorney general in Georgia without playing games?

Our next slap in the face came from the parole and pardon board. In Georgia, the governor has no jurisdiction over them. We contacted the parole and pardon board. Edward DuBose knew the chairman, James Donaldson, and had a relationship with him and thought he might be willing to listen to our presentation.

Edward DuBose arranged a meeting for us. We had arrived there the night before. We got up early so we could locate his office. The building had a breezeway. It was weird finding the office, because it was in that breezeway. There were Anita, Edward DuBose, a local minister, Rev. Singletary, attorney Al McSurely, Rev. Barber, and me. Edward had already talked to Donaldson. We were the team.

I am AME Zion. It turns out Donaldson's secretary was an AME Zion minister, and she had just gotten her church. We knew a lot of the same people. I explained about John. She knew before the committee knew. I felt as if we were going somewhere. I just knew I was in. We got to talking about the Zions and how they had changed. I really felt good about it. I thought after we left she might have a way to talk to Donaldson to help him understand that.

The first thing Donaldson did when he met with us was tell us a lie. He said, "We do not have the authority to grant a pardon."

I couldn't believe what I was hearing so I asked, "What?"

That was why we were there. The whole team began to question him hard until he finally said, "Well, better get the attorney." We tag-teamed him. We targeted him. We gave him no room to move.

They called in James Donaldson's attorney. The attorney came in. We were pressing Donaldson and he knew he had lied. He was up a tree. What could he do? The attorney said it had not been done in so many years. So I asked him if he were saying it cannot be done or had not been done? His answer was heartbreaking. "I am sure it can be done but the chances are zero to one percent," the attorney told us. We left the meeting heading back to North Carolina pissed off. We had come all this way. How could the parole and pardon chairman see a case like John's and overlook it?

Then I thought about all of the cases the parole and pardon board overlooked that had merit, like the Troy Davis case. Troy Davis was tried and executed in Georgia when there was great evidence that he was not guilty of the crime. He had the support of the Pope and former President Jimmy Carter. Former Congressman Bob Barr was opposed to taking that man's life. Nothing mattered. They still killed him. I guess there was no reason I should have been hopeful at that meeting. I guess I hoped deep down they were regretful about Troy Davis and would look favorably on John. They were not regretful. They did not look favorably at John. The sad part about it was it was a majority African-American board. So many times the reason an African-American is set up in a certain place is because they won't shake things up. Nobody can say the decision is racist when they have a minority who makes the decision. And many of them know the minute they say anything that questions the status quo, they will no longer have that seat or place.

There was a board meeting conference in Arlington, Virginia, with the national NAACP and the press department, and Anita was on that interview. She sold it. It was powerful; everybody was crying. That was the seal that brought national attention. That was John's fourth year in prison. But still we had an uphill battle. We had bad press in Georgia.

James Johnson was not out of the Wilson County jail yet, and we had John in prison. I had this idea that we would put them together. James and John both locked up in an unfair system. Neither of them had any problems with the law before. One had been successfully educated and the other was on his way. James would follow the footsteps of John. So biblically, we were going to tie them together. Rev. Barber said no, we had to keep them separate.

He was right. It was enough focusing on one. It was too difficult to put them together. So we worked on them both, separately. Fortunately we were able to get James released and then we focused solely on John.

James never went to trial. But John had a trial and was in prison which was much harder. I will tell anyone the most phenomenal thing we were able to do was to sell John's case to white people in Wilson. That was exactly what we had to do because we had just been painted as the devil in James's case. We were good people and John was a good man who had been wrongly accused

During that James Johnson case I recall standing on the courthouse steps with people who I considered my political allies, and they would go across the street to Wilson Hardware and take pictures. It didn't bother me because I knew the cause was right.

So we had to come out from under that weight and sell John, when in that case he had shot and killed a white man, and it seemed impossible. Georgia State Representative Tyrone Brooks, who is a civil rights activist, was sentenced recently to a year and a day in federal prison. He's seventy years old. He was framed. Tyrone was one of the people who came aboard to help John. He was there with us at the rallies.

There was a *Wilson Times* reporter named Sarah Thuerk. She wanted to go to interview John. She never got the chance to do that. She was very instrumental in letting people in Wilson know what was going on. I give her a lot of credit. She left the newspaper.

When Edward DuBose was on board with us, he was tough. He did all he could to help. We needed him. I went to Georgia at least once a month to work on the case. I would not get a chance to see John every time I went there, but I talked to him most days. That was a hard thing to do. John had become mistrustful. He just didn't trust anyone, including me.

When John was in solitary, I didn't know what to think. Anita kept me grounded during those times. That first time was awful. She would say, "John is a big boy. He knows how to take care of himself." But it was terrible because we had no idea what was going on. We would call and get no answers. If you ever have any type of communications with the corrections in Georgia, it is the most unethical institution—unconcerned about their inmates, unconcerned about a person's life—that I have ever dealt with. I cannot believe the lack of humanity that is prevalent in that system. I am sure it is mirrored in many prison systems, but I am talking about what I have encountered. I have dealt with Georgia and I know what the hell Georgia is about. When you call, they send you from one person to another— and, worse, they killed you with the cost. You'd hear the operator say, "You've got one minute." I would hang up when they would say fifteen seconds because I could not allow them to cut me off. I refused to let them hang up on me. When they did hang up, you couldn't call back. I can't imagine how John must have felt.

It was torture. When you start the call, it is supposed to be fifteen minutes. Then you have all of this automation, and by the time you actually talk to the person you only have ten minutes. It was close to $30 a call for that short amount of time on the phone.

The habeas was a victory for us. It was as if they were saying, We will dangle a carrot in front of you. You can see it, but you can't touch it. We were counting the thirty days, and they waited until the last day to file a response. What a rollercoaster. Every day you wonder. We hoped they would say they had done enough—screwed him as much as they wanted to, so let him go. But no.

People got involved and helped us that you never would have expected, like Wilson's mayor, Bruce Rose. I will forever be indebted to him. What so ironic is I know what the white power structure thought of me—they didn't like me. I don't know if they thought I had horns or what?

With the problems I have had over the years, some of them unforgivable, here we were, fighting together. I never would have thought that.

Seeing Rev. William Barber and Mayor Bruce Rose standing arm in arm on WTVD at the airport as Anita was taken to Georgia to see John, I said, What is going on in America? It was wonderful that Mayor Bruce Rose got Jeff Chesson to fly Anita down there to see John. She just could not travel because she was in too much pain because of the cancer.

I still cry today when I think of the lovable Anita. She never faltered in her fight for John. She could not believe John was coming home as she lay in the hospital. She was used to Georgia's lying. We told her John was coming home. She could not hold up her head, but she looked at us. We told her she had won. He was coming home. We told her she could rest.

It was terrible for John to be in the hole, and for us to not know what in the world was happening to him. The first thing I thought after I found out that maybe they put him in there because somebody wanted him dead. Maybe he was in there to be protected. But I think about it again, and I am not sure.

Chapter 18: The Deal to Go Home

I was going back to Cobb County. My case was overturned September 25, 2012, for ineffective assistance of counsel. I had to wait for thirty days to see if the attorney general would appeal my case. If he had been honorable and not appealed it, I would have been able to leave that system by October 2012 to see Anita and be with her before she passed away February 2, 2013.

Each day, I waited to see what would happen. The first few days I wasn't sure. I was on pins and needles. I expected them to file the appeal in the first week, but nothing. It was too early to get excited. So then two weeks passed, and I was starting to feel like maybe they wouldn't appeal. By the third week, I was excited. It was all over the news, and inmates all over Atlanta heard my case was overturned. By the twentieth day, other inmates were excited too. By the twenty-fifth day, we thought we had hit the home stretch. Guys were telling me I was going home.

Guys who were never going home were not happy for me. After all, they would never see outside again. But the guys who had numbers were happy for me. They could see the day when they would max out or get paroled. I would get out before them, but they were excited for me.

The attorney general waited until the twenty-ninth day to appeal what would have vacated my sentence.

I got a call from my lawyer, Mark Yurachek. "Well, John, I got some bad news," he told me. Bad news seemed to be all the news I was getting. "They appealed it," Yurachek said. I just wanted to know what I had to do next.

He told me I would be in there until after the first of the year. This was October. That killed me. Killed my spirit. There is a cross between anger and hurt and hope and losing your breath. Lots of emotion. The news meant another Thanksgiving locked up. Another Christmas inside. The New Year, where people look for new beginnings, and I was still incarcerated.

I needed to get home to Anita. She told me the cancer was beginning to affect her whole body. "John, I am in pain," Anita told me. "They said it has affected my liver now." I am the husband, and I began to be her pillar of strength. I could not let her know how hurt I was. I covered the phone so she could not hear me cry. "John, are you still there?" Anita asked. I asked her to hold on, and I flushed the toilet. I got some water and put it on my face. I had to gather my strength. She needed me. I tried to reassure her that she would be alright. "Just take care of our sons," Anita said to me. "God has me. I will be alright. I have made it right with God."

When somebody says that to you, you know it will not be long.

I got one message from my attorney that the negotiation was for me to do twenty years and I would be finished with my sentence.

"First of all, I am innocent. Why would I want to do twenty years?" I asked.

"It is the best they could do," my attorney said. I hung up on him.

He wrote me a letter. I did not respond. Then I got a call. "They said they might be able to work a deal, but they have to talk to the district attorney," Yurachek told me.

Pat Head was the DA who filed charges against me nine months after the initial incident. It had been an election year; he had an opponent and wanted to look "tough on crime." He won that election.

Four years later Head was running again, and it was clear he was going to lose. Suddenly he was willing to talk with us, to improve his political standing on his way out. After all, with the national attention my case was getting, who would want to be

known as the DA who put an innocent man
in prison?

The new district attorney, Victor Reyn-
olds, since he knew Anita was dying, of-
fered to have me plead guilty to voluntary
manslaughter and I would get a sentence of
time served. I asked my attorney why I
should say yes to voluntary manslaughter
when I already had been found not guilty of
that charge at my original trial. His thinking was, get me out of prison and worry
about that detail later. So, that was my
way to get home to my beloved wife.

I said yes. I just wanted to make it home.
That was my bottom line. I was not going to
do twenty years if I could help it.

Then Anita died. I began to have second
thoughts about saying I was guilty of voluntary manslaughter. I believed even if it
went all the way to the U.S. Supreme
Court, I would have my case overturned
and get out, but it might take years to do
that.

Even though it was appealed, the conviction was overturned. As a result, I would go

back to the condition I was in before I was in prison, which is the county jail. They shipped me out quickly to Cobb County; they feared I would change my mind about the plea deal. When I got to Cobb County, the district attorney wanted to talk. Turns out *they* wanted to do this deal, not the attorney general. They wanted to protect themselves from a lawsuit.

Standing there in front of the judge with him asking me if I wanted to plead guilty to voluntary manslaughter, all I could do was laugh. What a mess. Voluntary manslaughter, time served and probation. Thirteen years of probation. Free, but not really free.

Chapter 19: Pleading Double Jeopardy to Get Out

I didn't sleep that night when I knew I had to go to court just after Anita died. Many nights I would doze and wake up. But I knew there was a lot going to happen and a lot was on the line. I could not really trust anyone. Anything could happen.

When I went into the courtroom, I didn't expect to see all of my hometown folks there. I was shackled and wore an orange jumpsuit that was so faded that it looked as if it were ten years old.

Walking in those chains you knew the inhumanity of what slaves went through. When you walk in them, it makes you kind of lean or tilt your body and take a half step. You can't walk with your normal stride. The chains swing back and forth to the rhythm of your shortened walk. You know you are a slave to the state when you have them on. You don't have a will of your own. They take it. You aren't expected to have a mind or to think. They do everything to take that from you, too, if they think you are dangerous.

Thinking gets you put in solitary. It seems they watch you to see if you are a thinker. They do allow you to be savage. I knew, as I was standing before the judge that morning, it was double jeopardy. I was going in there to plead guilty to voluntary manslaughter with time served, and I knew there would be thirteen years of probation. Nobody in America gets thirteen years of probation. It was double jeopardy.

When I walked into the courtroom that morning, there was media and friends—and some faces that were not so friendly. I could not worry about that. I was so emotional. I had just lost Anita.

The idea was for me to leave Georgia and go back to North Carolina. The details were already worked out. After waiting so many years, there was a real, slim possibility I could walk out that door. The reason I say slim possibility is because even though my attorney, Mark Yurachek, and I talked and supposedly everything was in place, you learn in prison to never count your chickens before they hatch. Any number of things could have prevented me from walking out the door that day.

If I could have just cut myself into thirds, the first part of me was excited, a second part was emotional and a third part was angry—all at the same time. We live in a great nation, the United States of America. I believed with all of my heart what happened to me was a modern-day lynching.

Brian Epp is who they accused me of killing, when he had actually killed himself. I gave a warning shot and, true enough, I did shoot him. But here is the thing we will probably never know and nobody will ever want to talk about: Had the medical examiner given us the correct results of the autopsy before we went to court—the results where the medical examiner tested him for methamphetamines—maybe there would have been a different result in the first trial. We don't know if the gunshot killed him, or if he had a cardiac arrest from the methamphetamines that were in his body. That never came out during the trial. It was only in the habeas corpus after research, and after private investigators searched for the truth, that we became aware there were drugs in his system.

I was to stand there in front of the judge and plead guilty to charges a jury had previously found me not guilty of. I knew my new deal was a deal with the devil. I had to consider my two sons, and I wanted to get back to my wife's remains. I wasn't in the courtroom yet and my mind and my body were racing. It was as if someone had lit a string of firecrackers and they were just firing at random. They escorted me up to the second-floor hallway, and there were the doors to the courtroom and the judge sitting there and the room full of people. My attorney, Yurachek, leaned over and said to me, "John, you are going home."

I took a breath. It was a shallow breath, not the long deep breath of relief you would expect. I said "Yes, but I am not totally free yet."

They took me back to Cobb County to get my papers and transcripts that I had. They actually put my prison garb into the bag of papers. I didn't want the prison clothes, but they will always be a reminder. It could be that someone in my family, some son or daughter down the line, may look at that uniform and know that if you put that on, you will be in a bad place. And there are no guarantees that you will ever get back out. It is only by the grace of God that I did get out with health and strength and a sound mind. I came out and knew that what happened to me could have happened to anybody else, but God chose me to be that vessel.

I think about Job in the Bible. He lost everything. God restored him. It is like being a modern-day Job. I'm not saying this because I want God to restore me, because he already has. He gave me a second chance. Being out is truly a second chance. I plan on making the best of it as long as I am here on earth.

When you go into a jail or prison, they book you in. When you are leaving, they take you through exiting. As some of the law enforcement were taking me through the steps to exit, they were wondering what all of the excitement was going on outside about me.

I remember one guard looked at me and said, "Are you some celebrity or something, all those people out there waiting on you?" There were jailers of different ranks coming up telling me there was a crowd waiting for me. I told them I wasn't a celebrity.

"When you become famous out there, don't forget about us," one guard said to me. I was thinking to myself, Isn't this something. You are the same people who treated me badly.

They allowed me to take a shower. I don't think they usually allow inmates to take showers up there where I was. It was where the officers take their showers.

When I first went into the prison system, I took a shower in the filthiest of showers. It looked as if it had never been cleaned. It had black greasy walls and floors. There was mold and discolored mildew all over the walls. Conversely, the shower when I exited the prison was almost immaculate. They actually gave me soap. In prison everything is cheap and low quality; anything from the outside is called "free-world" stuff and the products are better quality. For the first time in six years, I had Dial soap with fragrance. They gave me shampoo that smelled good. The water in the shower was warm and fresh like rain. As the water bounced off my body, I said, Lord, I thank you. It was not a baptism in the submersion way, but it was a cleansing—washing away all the filth of the past six years. I wanted to leave all of the dirt right there in that shower. For the first time in six years, I was taking a shower and not watching to see who was coming up to stab me. After six years, even though I was not outside of the prison yet, there was the sign of a better day ahead. There was the promise of going home and walking around freely. God had brought me this far. I began to cry in that shower. I was in that prison, but I was free to cry as the warm water covered me.

Then reality came with a tap on the door. "All right. We are waiting on you," one voice said. So, I got myself together. I had requested a charcoal gray suit, and Frank Jones brought me one. The guard brought me the suit.

While my loved ones waited hours and hours for me to come through the door, and while the guards were supposedly wishing me well, they were running more background checks on me. I am sure they wanted to find something somewhere so they would have a reason to keep me there. There are many John McNeils in the country. I have never had any run-ins with law enforcement, so there was nothing to find anywhere in the country. Eventually, they called me, and I signed for my things.

I took those first steps to walk out of the prison February 12, 2013. When I turned the corner, I saw the people standing there. I couldn't explain the sensation that came upon me at that moment, seeing family and friends waiting for me. My heart was pounding so hard it seemed my shirt should have been shaking. I had a lot of conflicting emotions. I wanted to run into everyone's arms. I wanted to stand there and cry. I was trembling with emotion. And I was scared. Then as I walked up, they all rushed me. I wanted to run away from everybody at the same time. But to run back into the prison where they held me captive for six years was not where I wanted to be. I thought, I will take my chances with these guys who want to hug me.

I also wanted to tell everyone the mean things that happened to me. I prayed when I was in prison and attended religious services. But when Rev. William Barber of the North Carolina NAACP began praying for me, as is customary in situations like that, I could not close my eyes.

People were gathered around me tight. That scared me and it was uncomfortable. They were touching me because they were so happy for me to be out. Intellectually I knew I was out of prison, but realistically I had just gotten out moments before. It made me flinch when I would feel a hand touch me. It made every hair on my body stand on end. When I was in prison, you just didn't touch anybody. I talk to you. You talk to me. Don't put your hands on me. In prison, if you put your hands on a person, it means going to war with that person. You are trying to hurt me or kill me. That was the mentality inside the prison. It was the new normal I had learned in prison. And here I was with these wonderful people who had fought for me, raised money and prayed for me and saw me to this day. All they wanted to do was touch me. Closing your eyes when you are surrounded like that is not something you would do in prison. It was not a safe thing to do. You cannot trust any person in prison. So, I watched while they prayed. Trust, or lack of trust, didn't allow me to be comfortable enough with my new surroundings to close my eyes for prayer. I don't remember what was said in the prayer. There were too many things going on in my head. I was going home, but not to my wife Anita waiting to embrace me. I was going to look at her body in a casket. I was going to be with her too late. I wanted to be there when she was alive. I wanted to hold her hand. All of that was taken from me. I wanted to see my mother. That was not going to happen. I had so many things I had to think about. What was going to happen? Glad to be free and scared at the same time. I wasn't scared enough to go back inside, but there was a kind of fear.

After the prayer, somebody asked me what I was going to do now. "Breathe freedom" was all I could say. There were so many cameras and I really didn't have anything to say at that time. The words were just not there. I wanted to smile. I hope I managed a smile at the people. My oldest brother took my arm and walked me to the car. I was thinking, Let's get out of here. Out of here was not leaving Georgia. I had to go to Cobb County to see the probation folks. There was a carful of us: Rev. William Barber, Frank Jones, and Charles Cook from North Carolina. The probation officers were rude. There were two white women and a black lady.

"Get out and go sit in the car," one lady said to Rev. Barber and the rest. They all wanted to be nice, so they turned to walk out. One of them tried to grab Cook's camera. The probation officer said, "This is not a place to take pictures."

I said, "I signed the paperwork they asked me to." Then I headed back to the car and got in.

All I wanted to see was Georgia in the rearview mirror. At that moment, I knew I would never live in Georgia again; at that moment, I didn't even want to see it on a map. Just cut that state out. We should see Florida, South Carolina, North Carolina. But Georgia was still not ready to see me free. I got a call from my attorney telling me we had problems. I put him on speakerphone. "John, you've got to turn around. They said you can't leave the state of Georgia. And everybody in that car that crosses the state line will be thrown in jail, too."

So we pulled over right away. I knew it! The judge said I could go back home to North Carolina. It was in the ruling. You can't trust anyone. Here we are on the side of the road in the state that I could hate. Now it was well after 5 p.m. All offices were officially closed. So at this time, those who were in the car got on the phone with some NAACP attorneys, who called the Georgia attorney general and the governor of Georgia. They knew somebody who knew somebody. I know my heart was beating, but there was this ache. I was filled with dread. I began to wonder if it was a sign they were going to tell me I had to stay in Georgia. I didn't want to spend another minute in that state, and I couldn't have been in more misery just waiting. Later we got another call from Yurachek, my attorney. "Wow, John. I see you know people in high places. They say you can go to North Carolina now."

My heart could beat normally again. So we came on through to North Carolina. No stopping except for gas. When I got back to North Carolina, there were so many media outlets at my mother-in-law's house that I could not greet my family like I had intended. I was driven around, and we ended up at the Holiday Inn near the hospital.

Frank went in and got the room, and I used another entrance to get in. A woman spotted me and kept looking at me. I wondered if she knew who I was. I didn't want to talk to anyone at that time. I got into my room, but I could not sleep at all that night. I was so emotional, and I was in a hotel room, not a prison cell. I peeped out of the peephole in the door of the hotel room, and that lady stopped right outside of my door. I took a chair and placed it under the doorknob to jam the door. And I walked the floor all night. I had phone numbers if I wanted to talk to someone. But it was like going through withdrawal.

I was alone with my thoughts of Anita and my sons and all that had happened.

That day had been filled with excitement. From an orange prison jumpsuit to a charcoal gray suit. From chains on my wrists and my ankles, being kept in a cell, to a hotel room with no bars, no sounds, no screaming, no crying, just quiet. I walked the floor until about 5 a.m.

I sat down on the side of the bed. I lay with my upper body sideways on the bed and my feet on the floor. I could not lie down in that bed. I never took off my suit. I was still battling with the cells I had been kept in. I thought at any moment guards or other inmates would crash open the door. I was ready for war. I only wanted to rest my body. I never realized I had gone to sleep. The next thing I knew, the phone was ringing telling me to take a shower and come on downstairs.

It was a bittersweet homecoming with Anita gone. I went to the church and there were so many people there. I thought about all of the people who helped me. All of the people God put in my path. I talked to Anita a day before she died. She was so weak and in so much pain. I told her not to talk. "I just want to hear you breathe," I said to her. I just listened to her breath, no words. I pressed the phone so hard to my ear listening that it left indentions to my ear and face. I could not miss a moment. I understood things were changing forever, because I was breathing for her, and for myself.

When I was released from prison, that's where I got "breathe freedom." Anita's breathing was the same as mine. Her breathing freedom was going to a greater place. I was coming back to the same place. Her freedom was leaving her temple. I was breathing to come back to this temple.

In life you want your loved ones to live forever. I thought she would live forever. I recaptured in my mind all of the years from my teens with the sassy Anita, to our twenties, then thirties, then forties. Can you imagine all of that time running rapidly through my mind? It was like watching a film on fast-forward. All those years took time, but at that moment they all ran so rapidly through my mind it made my emotions hard to deal with. It was like an ocean wave that hits you and knocks you up in the air.

When I closed my eyes, I could see her smile. My mind took me back to a time when we went to that Hardee's on Hines Street and we didn't have much money, but we had enough for one hamburger. We split that hamburger and one small fry. We left there and we went walking. Those are the times I remember most.

Later in life, we had money, things and good times. But the times I remember most are the times when she and I didn't have anything. We had each other and love. She was my love and that is why I decided to bury her on Valentine's Day. I talked it over with Frank Jones, and I could have done it on the thirteenth, but I wanted it on the same day that lovers celebrate their love for each other. It will be the most memorable Valentine's of my life. I dream about Anita when I'm asleep. She still talks to me in my dreams. I'm not back to myself yet, and she talks to me, helping me. I don't talk to her in my dreams, I just listen. I don't want to miss what she is saying. Funny, it seems she is really with me until I wake up and see it was all a dream. I thank God he allows her to visit me in my dreams.

Chief Justice Leah Ward Sears's Dissent

Under OCGA § 16-3-21(a), McNeil was justified in shooting Epp "only if he . . . reasonably believe[d] that such force [wa]s necessary to prevent death or great bodily injury to himself . . . or to prevent the commission of a forcible felony." At trial, the State had the burden to disprove McNeil's affirmative defense of justification beyond a reasonable doubt. On appeal, in reviewing the sufficiency of the evidence, we must view the evidence in the light most favorable to the verdict, and determine whether a rational trier of fact could have found the absence of self-defense beyond a reasonable doubt. I con-

clude that, viewing the evidence in the light most favorable to the verdict, no rational trier of fact could have found the absence of self-defense beyond a reasonable doubt.

At the outset, I note that McNeil was not under a duty to retreat either when he drove onto his property or when Epp charged him by coming from the neighbor's property onto McNeil's property. Although the majority correctly states that McNeil told the 911 operator that he wanted to "whip [Epp's] ass" and that McNeil retrieved a gun from his glove compartment, in analyzing whether the evidence is sufficient to support the verdict, the majority fails to acknowledge that the undisputed evidence shows that the shooting occurred on McNeil's property, that McNeil never left his property, that Epp was on a neighbor's property when McNeil drove into his driveway, and that Epp left the neighbor's property and crossed over the neighbor's yard and onto McNeil's property. As for whether McNeil could have reasonably believed that deadly force was necessary, the majority also fails to acknowledge that Bob-

by Smith, a neutral witness, testified that McNeil was on his property and in his driveway when Epp began approaching him from the neighbor's yard. Smith added that McNeil fired a shot into the ground and verbally warned Epp not to come any closer. According to Smith, despite these warnings, Epp increased his speed in moving toward McNeil. McNeil's son testified that Epp pulled a knife on him in his own backyard, that he told his father this, and that Epp rushed at McNeil from the next door neighbor's yard. McNeil gave testimony that was similar in relevant respects to that given by his son and Smith, and he added that Epp reached into his truck and put something in his right pocket before he rushed toward McNeil and onto his property.

McNeil's call to 911 reporting that Epp had pulled a knife on his son supports the veracity of La'Ron's and McNeil's testimony. Significantly, the police did find a knife in Epp's right pocket. Further supporting the testimony of McNeil, his son, and Smith that Epp was the aggressor was the testimony of

David Samson and Libby Jones to the effect that Epp had behaved in an extremely aggressive and inappropriate manner toward them concerning problems with Epp's work on their house. Although the State had the burden to disprove self-defense, the State did not offer any evidence to rebut McNeil's evidence that Epp was the aggressor, that Epp came onto McNeil's property from a neighbor's yard despite being told previously that he did not have permission to do so, that McNeil knew that Epp had threatened to stab his son moments earlier, and that Epp had a knife on his person when he charged McNeil. In fact, the only witness called by the State who actually saw the shooting, Bobby Smith, gave testimony that actually supported McNeil's evidence that Epp was the aggressor.

Even viewed in the light most favorable to the verdict, the evidence was overwhelming in showing that a reasonable person in McNeil's shoes would have believed that he was subject to an imminent physical attack by an aggressor possessing a knife and that it was necessary to use deadly force to protect himself from serious bodily injury or a forcible felony. Under the facts of this case, it would be unreasonable to require McNeil to wait until Epp succeeded in attacking him, thereby potentially disarming him, getting control of the gun, or stabbing him before he could legally employ deadly force to defend himself. This is not what Georgia law requires. To the contrary,

[i]t is not essential to justify a homicide that there should be an actual assault made upon th[e] defendant. Threats accompanied by menaces, though the menaces do not amount to an actual assault, may in some instances be sufficient to arouse a reasonable belief that one's life is in imminent danger or that one is in imminent danger of great bodily harm or that a forcible felony is about to be committed upon one's person.

I share the majority's reluctance to overturn a jury verdict. However, I conclude that no rational trier of fact could find, based on the evidence presented at trial, that the State disproved McNeil's claim of self-defense beyond a reasonable doubt. Accordingly, I must dissent.

Chapter 20: Home Isn't Home

When I got home to Wilson, North Carolina, I was so happy to be out of prison that I let my guard down. It was almost thirty years since I'd left. I thought, Wow, this feels good. People began to want to do things for me and I was so happy to be home and have such a warm welcome. They wanted to take me out to dinner and lunch and show me love. Somewhere along the line, I came up short.

After I got home from prison, I was poisoned four times. Two of those times, I was told if I'd had just a little more of that poison, it would have taken me out. I was very ill. One time I called my soon-to-be-wife, Teresa, and said I need to go to the doctor's office, which was out of town. I had stuff coming out of my ears and everywhere. I was so weak I could hardly hold my head up. That's how bad it was. The CDC said it was a case of poisoning. I recall the two places where it happened. My guard went back up. When you look at it, sometimes it's the people who are the closest who can hurt you. It was like when Judas betrayed Jesus.

After the first two times, I began to catch things. I was back with keen senses like when I was in prison. I got death threats from the time I was arrested to when I got out and moved to Wilson. Someone loosened four of the lug nuts on my car. I had to travel thirty to forty minutes to get home. By the grace of God, the wheels didn't come off. I do not know to this day who or how many people tried to hurt me after my release.

I still protect myself from people. I don't know if I will ever be able to fully relax. I know now that this is a dangerous world. You have to be on the square and you can't slip. The wall I have up will probably be there until I die. I never know who will come after me. I don't want to be Monday-morning quarterbacking.

The state of Georgia changed my life. There are times when I want to just relax and the smallest thing will remind me to bring the shield back up. This is my new norm. However, after a few years out of prison, some of those pains from the past have faded, but many are still here. I don't think I'll ever go back to who I was before.

Our country has come a long way, but there is a long way to go for the cloak of justice to wrap around the poor, those who are of color and those without political clout. We still struggle with race in the twenty-first century. Too many churchgoers are bigots and racists while claiming to be Christians. So many people still think that if a person is in prison they have shed their humanity and are nothing but a monster rightfully kept in a cage.

I believe God is calling on us all to do better. I know that good can conquer evil and love is greater than hate. My hope remains in God. When one goes through the fire and is delivered out the other side into a new understanding of their very being, it's nothing less than a gift from God.

After a few years out of prison, feelings of strangeness, confusion, fear, and disorientation are being displaced by a sense of awe and reverence, which has helped me to understand that with the death of the man I was has come the blessing of new beginnings and that such new beginnings are the opportunities for returning that gift back to God.

The man I now seek to be embraces these new beginnings and prays for grace, for an ever-greater understanding of forgiveness as the way forward into healing, and this healing must be for all who may hold thoughts of anger, retribution, hate, harm and hurt. The man I seek now to be also prays for wisdom to see how these understandings are to be expressed—in loving service not only to those in the community who nurtured me, and to which I am blessed to return, but to all on this earth.

—John McNeil, 2019

JUSTICE for John McNeil

"An Englishman's Home Is His Castle"

SIR EDWARD COKE, ENGLISH JURIST (1552-1634)

"In Georgia, a Black Man's Home Is Nothing."

REV. DR. WILLIAM J. BARBER II, N.C. NAACP PRESIDENT (2005-PRESENT) AND NATIONAL NAACP BOARD MEMBER

John McNeil at his house in Georgia

Intake photo at Baldwin State Prison

*Anita McNeil speaking on John's behalf at
the NAACP national headquarters*

Anita at the NAACP national headquarters

*Exiting prison. From left: Frank Jones, John McNeil,
Rev. William Barber*

From left: Edward DuBose, Chris McNeil, Rev. William Barber, John, Robert McNeil Jr.

Press conference at Cobb County Detention Center

John speaking at Anita's church in Wilson, NC
Inset: Anita and John's anniversary celebration

www.ingramcontent.com/pod-product-compliance
Lightning Source LLC
Chambersburg PA
CBHW021823090426

42811CB00032B/1991/J